Dare to Love

The Art of Merging Science and Love Into
Parenting Children with Difficult Behaviors

ALSO BY HEATHER FORBES

Beyond Consequences, Logic and Control, Volume 1

Beyond Consequences, Logic and Control, Volume 1, Spanish Edition

Beyond Consequences, Logic and Control, Volume 2

100 Daily Parenting Reflections

Check out the
Beyond Consequences Institute
website today:
■

- Sign-up on our network and receive announcements of future free events such as webinars and lectures.

- Receive Heather's free eNewsletter for more Q&A support.

- Download free articles that will further your understanding of the Beyond Consequences Model.

- Learn how you can have Heather T. Forbes, LCSW in your area to hold a seminar or workshop.

- Purchase additional copies of this book for teachers, friends, and family members.

- View videos of how this model works when parents make the commitment to move from fear to love.

www.beyondconsequences.com

Dare to Love

The Art of Merging Science and Love Into
Parenting Children with Difficult Behaviors

Heather T. Forbes, LCSW

Beyond Consequences Institute

Dare to Love

The Art of Merging Science and Love Into Parenting Children with Difficult Behaviors

Copyright © 2009 by Heather T. Forbes

ISBN 0-9777040-6-8

First Edition 2009

Published by:
Beyond Consequences Institute, LLC
Boulder, CO

Book Design:
Tyler Thomas

Dedication

∎

*This book is dedicated to
my amazing children,*

JOANNA AND BEN

*I love you with all my heart.
May you always know
with complete 100% certainty
that love does exist in this world.*

Table of Contents

■

A Note to the Reader
.

"Love Never Fails." It is easy to say these three words–*love never fails*–without truly thinking about it. "Well, of course love never fails," you think automatically. Yet when you are raising a child with difficult or severe behaviors, you live each day at a level of fear that your child is NOT going to be okay.

What if you could believe, without a doubt, that love really never fails? How would this change your everyday interactions with not just your child, but with everybody you met? Can you imagine the peace and calm you would experience everyday if you lived out of a paradigm of confidence and reassurance that love really is enough?

Stop for a minute. Take a breath and say that phrase again very slowly: **Love Never Fails.** Soak it in completely. It isn't just a header on my website or a slogan on a T-shirt. From the depth of fear that I used to live out of and from the fear I had for my own children's well being when they were younger, I can now unequivocally, without hesitation and from the depth of my soul, say that love never fails.

Through my experience as a professional in the mental health field, but more importantly, through my experience as a mother, I have come not only to know, but to witness the power of love. Love has the power to heal and it has the power to change chaos into calm. Love can move someone from a screaming rage to gut-wrenching tears. Love can touch someone for a moment yet last for an entire lifetime.

As humans, we have allowed our life experiences to shift us from living out of a state of love and into a state of fear. This state of fear has now become what we consider "normal." It has become easier for us to live in a state of fear instead of a state of love.

Think about that. It is easier to live in a state of fear than in a state of love! Yet, concurrently, we stay on this perpetual quest to find peace and happiness in our lives.

How can this be? Why is it easier to live in a place of fear than in a place of love? Is it that fear has become so familiar it brings a level of certainty while love is so unfamiliar that it is hard to trust and believe in it?

We enter into the world in a state of love but as "life happens" and we are neither supported nor loved unconditionally, we shift our love programs to fear programs. As children, it is hard for us to maintain a framework of love when everyone around us, our parents, relatives, teachers–our entire culture–is living in a place of fear.

Every moment a child is born, we need to celebrate because with the birth of every child comes a new chance for us to break this fear cycle. Children come into this world to return us back to our original state of love. They bring to us the essence of who we are designed to be.

Unfortunately, the majority of parenting models available to us speak to quite the opposite. These models tell us that the parent is the one with the knowledge and wisdom; that the parent is the teacher and the child is the student. The reality is completely opposite. In truth, our children are our teachers and we are the students.

■

In truth, our children are our teachers and we are the students.

■

It is easy to see this when we interact with a baby. The baby looks at us with his big bright eyes, smiles at us, and simply radiates love. However, it is hard to see this love when our teenager is cussing at us, telling us that he hates us, and that we never do anything for him. Where is the love in that?

We cannot see the love because we are focused solely on the *behavior*. As parents, we stay fixated on how our child is acting, rather than on how our child is feeling. We take their behavior personally and instead of connecting with their emotional state, we react to them from our fear, justifying this by saying that the child needs to learn good manners, needs to be respectful to his parents, and that we are teaching the child to be responsible.

In reality, what we are teaching our child is how to stay in a state of fear, not how to shift to a state of love. It is time to stop the cycle. It is time to stop the generational train of living in a place of fear and not trusting that love never fails. At a physical, emotional, and spiritual level, fear is not a natural state. Perpetual states of fear and stress are the main causes of disease and mental illness.

■

In reality, what we are teaching our child is how to stay in a state of fear, not how to shift to a state of love.

■

When raising children, especially children with difficult behaviors, we need to dig deeper within ourselves to find the love it takes to overcome the fear. It will take us believing that our children are communicating something profound and important through their behaviors. They are giving us the answers through their behaviors. It is up to us to start "listening" to their behaviors.

It will take trusting in the power of love and trusting that your child actually wants to please you more than anyone on this planet. It will take trusting that it can be as simple as staying present with your child, listening to him, and simply connecting with him in order for him to calm down and shift his behaviors and attitudes.

This takes courage because it will take shifting to an entirely new paradigm-an entirely new belief system. Some people won't even change their hairstyles much less their paradigm for living! So I encourage you to make your move and dare to love. Dare to love your child unconditionally through his behaviors; not just before or after his behaviors, but during. Your child needs to know what it feels like to be unconditionally loved when he is in his rawest and most dysregulated state. This is the healing moment and the moment of opportunity for the deepest parent/child connection to develop.

This book is divided up into two parts. First, the science behind what we now know about affect regulation and how the brain operates is explained. The second part of the book describes, through a series of questions and answers, the art of merging both science and love into unconditional parenting.

I would not present this material to you if I did not believe 100% from my heart and soul that this parenting paradigm will move your family from a state of frustration, chaos, and turmoil to a state of enjoyment, love, and fulfillment. I have seen it work both professionally and in my own family. Be sure to refer to the dual series of *Beyond Consequences, Logic, and Control (Volumes 1 and 2)* for the foundational principles to this parenting paradigm. *Dare to Love* is designed to give you more applications to the principles described in those two previous books.

The time is now. Stop the negative cycling and return back to love. It *is* possible. Find the courage to do something different and dare to love your children from a place of unconditional acceptance, free of fear, free of judgment, and full of relationship!

Press on,

Heather T. Forbes, LCSW

A Life-Transforming Offer!

My heart and soul has been poured into the following pages, along with years of research, experience, hurt, and joy. You have worked hard to find answers for your child, and I don't want to waste your time or money. For the time you take to study this book thoroughly and put the ideas into place, I'd like to offer you a day of transformation … a coupon for two to attend any one of my upcoming Beyond Consequences Live seminars – free. If you've enjoyed this book, you'll love the live seminar. To redeem the discount, just bring your copy of the book to the seminar. Sign-up online at: **www.BeyondConsequencesLive.com**

This is good for the attendance of one single parent and support person, or one couple. Valid only after the purchase of the book. Book must be shown at the seminar.

Upcoming Locations:
Los Angeles, CA
San Francisco, CA
Dallas, TX
Denver, CO
Chicago, IL
St. Louis, MO
Atlanta, GA

For more information, log on to: www.BeyondConsequencesLive.com

Finally, here's my 100% guarantee to you:
If, after putting into place any of the ideas in this book for a consistent period of two weeks, you do not see at least a 50 percent reduction in your child's negative behavior, return the book to me and I will refund every penny of your money, no questions asked!

However, if what you try works, send me an e-mail letting me know what you tried, how it worked, and how long it took for you to see results. Just e-mail me at info@beyondconsequences.com. I am serious about you, your child, and your family, but most of all, I am serious when I say that love never fails!

PART ONE

Creating a New Understanding

CHAPTER ONE

Asking the Right Question

After reading parenting book after parenting book, I have come to one very important conclusion. We have been asking the wrong question. We have been asking, "How do I get my child to change his behavior?" The focus has been on moving a child from negative behavior to positive behavior. You know the routine: sticker charts, taking away privileges, responding only to nice talk, rewarding good behavior with a prize or that treasured new toy, and the like. Are these working? Do they create lasting change or do you find yourself constantly digging into your bag of "tricks" to find something new and innovative because the old techniques are not working anymore? Or worse, do you find that all those tricks and techniques you try actually make the situation between you and your child worse?

Ask the wrong question and you will get the wrong answer. This is why those sticker charts are not working. In order to get the solution we need to start asking the right question. Children are emotional beings. They are deeply emotional and spiritual creatures that we have somehow come to view as "little rational and logical thinking adults." But this is not who they are.

The right question needs to stem from the understanding that children operate from an emotional platform, not a behavioral framework. Thus, the question we need to start asking ourselves is,

"What is *driving* my child's behavior?"

When we begin to ask this question, we switch our focus to that which is at the core of our children's negative behavior. At this core is a state of fear, pain, and/or overwhelm that comes from a child being outside of his window of stress tolerance. Children do not act out from a conscious place. It goes much deeper than this.

As adults, we have shifted into a place of intellect, rationalization, and logical thinking because it is a safer place from which to operate. Logic is much more predictable than emotions, thus more comfortable. As human beings, we have a need for certainty. This certainty is found through intellectual thinking and rational thought. For many of us, our childhood experiences moved us into this realm of thinking because feelings of anger, fear, and sadness became unsafe and people got either emotionally and/or physically hurt.

This is exactly why children are in our lives. They are our examples to return us back to our natural state of emotional living. This is where life exists at a deeper and more meaningful level. We find our purpose and our passion for who we are and the reason we are on this planet when we operate out of a state of emotional expression and capture the essence of what distinguishes us from all other mammals on this planet.

Our children are in our lives to challenge us to *Dare to Love* again. In order to connect with who they are, we must shift ourselves back to living from love, not fear; living from emotional expression, not logical thought; and learning the difference between unconditional love and conditional love.

Effective and rewarding parenting takes going beyond the behaviors, beyond dishing out consequences, beyond thinking logically, and beyond trying to control our children. It takes putting love into action in a whole new way and connecting with your child at a deep, intrinsic level—a whole new dimension of parenting.

Switching your thinking from a behavioral framework to a love-based framework that is focused on emotional connection, will not be easy. Daring to love your children beyond consequences, logic, and control, will take courage, faith, commitment, and follow through.

When you learn how to put unconditional love into action, you have the power to change *any* family situation. Parenting through power and authority over our children comes from fear and ultimately undermines a child's ability to trust and relate to both themselves and others. Conversely, parenting through unconditional love and relationship equips our children to develop their own internal sense of control and empowers them to enter the world with a strong sense of self, well-developed love for self, and an ability to relate to others through tolerance, patience, and understanding. It simply starts by asking the right question: "What is driving my child's behavior?

CHAPTER TWO

The Emotional Core
■

Cognitive and behavioral parenting approaches simply are not working with our children, especially children with difficult and severe behaviors. Currently, there are over five million children on drugs for psychiatric and behavioral issues. This is a 400 percent increase in psychotropic drug prescriptions to children in a 10 year period. When we read statistics such as these it is time to question these traditional approaches.

Researchers are showing that, "In adults as well as children, emotions are the central medium through which vital information, especially information about interpersonal relations is transmitted and received." *(Dorpat, Psychoanalystic Inquiry, 2001)* In an article in *Motivation and Emotion (2007)*, Ryan points out that, "After three decades of the dominance of cognitive approaches, motivational and emotional processes have roared back into the limelight." We are living in a time period where we need to recognize that emotions do "matter" in areas such as healthcare, education, sports, religion, and especially parenting. Parenting is where it all begins.

Originally, Freud partitioned the mind into two parts, the conscious and the unconscious. In the last two decades, brain science has expanded on this concept to show that the brain is divided into the left hemisphere and the right hemisphere. Verbal, conscious, and serial informational processing happens in the left hemisphere while nonverbal, unconscious, and emotional processing happens in the right hemisphere. The right hemisphere is the emotional brain that drives human behavior. This is the essential characteristic of what makes us uniquely human.

■
The right hemisphere is the emotional brain that drives human behavior.
■

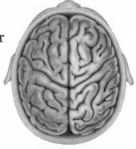

Left Hemisphere
- Conscious processor
- Language
- Analytical thought
- Logic

Right Hemisphere
- Unconscious processor
- Intuition
- Emotional self
- Imagination

With this perspective, it is clear that children (as well as adults) transmit and receive information through their emotions. Life experiences and behavioral decisions stem from the right hemisphere, the emotional self. Dr. Allan Schore's work shows that the right hemisphere filters and appraises our life's experiences and that our response is influenced by how our right hemisphere interprets the event. The right hemisphere dominates the left hemisphere's logical and analytical thought processes.

Children (as well as adults) transmit and receive information through their emotions.

Additionally, the previous scientific practice of viewing the unconscious mind as a static memory bank that influenced our actions has been replaced. Current clinical models now refer to the unconscious as "relational unconscious," meaning that we respond not from our own individual thoughts but from the interaction between us and another person. These relational interactions happen through right-brain to right-brain emotional communications. They happen through the parent/child relationship at the emotional level.

This is a call to rethink our parenting. Traditionally, parenting has been left-brain to left-brain interactions. We have been instructing our children, "If you do this behavior, then I will implement this as a consequence." Such typical interactions stem solely from rational and logical thinking, void of emotional expressions, completely ignoring the dominate influence of the right hemisphere. If we align our parenting with science, it will mean shifting our communication to the emotional level.

Fear and Trauma

Fear is an important emotion to understand in human behavior, especially in terms of parenting. Fear is not conscious experience. Fearful responses happen when we are not even conscious of being afraid.

In response to an event we experience, our right hemisphere responds faster than our left hemisphere. The left hemisphere, after the initial response from the right hemisphere, will then perform a more correct and organized analysis of the event. Because the right hemisphere's "first on the spot" response happens prior to the left-hemisphere's interpretation, the signals are more physiological. The right hemisphere is directly connected to the body, and thus, our reactions of fear happen at the body level.

For a child whose negative behaviors are more intense, more frequent, and less responsive to traditional parenting techniques, we must consider the child's earlier history of experiencing fear. Most likely, this child experienced a higher level of fear and is acting from an even deeper unconscious level of fear than other children. It is fear at the body level created from traumatic experiences.

We underestimate how life experiences influence a child's response system and have been reluctant as a society to recognize how prevalent trauma is in children's lives. Trauma is simply any threatening event that puts us in a state of being overwhelmed by fear, helplessness, and terror. In the past, the idea of trauma was limited to events that were "news noteworthy" such as 9/11, earthquakes, fires, and other significant events. Peter Levine, an expert in the understanding of trauma, states "trauma is the most avoided, ignored, denied, misunderstood, and untreated cause of human suffering." *(Levine, Healing Trauma, 2005)*

For a child, trauma can happen in what most adults consider normal life events. Falling off a bicycle can be traumatic for a child, if at that moment the child feels overwhelmed and in danger. Even more overlooked is trauma that happens at the emotional level for children. This is when a child experiences the lack of consistent love, affection, attunement, caring, understanding, and protection from a parent or parent figure. When a child feels like he was the cause of his parent's divorce, feels like he is not special in his parent's eyes, or feels like he is an interruption to the parent's day, is when *real* trauma happens to children.

It is not the event itself that defines the trauma, but rather the emotional experience of fear during the event. This emotional experience happens in the right hemisphere. This part of the brain contains a well-defined network for rapidly responding to danger and other problems that are perceived as urgent. It initiates self-protective responses such as avoidance, escape, and retaliation. Schutz (2005) describes this emotionality as the right brain's "red phone" to handle urgent matters without delay.

> ■
>
> *It is not the event itself that defines the trauma, but rather the emotional experience of fear during the event that defines the trauma.*
>
> ■

Children engaged fully in this response system have erroneously been interpreted as children with "bad behavior." While all along, according to this new evidence, they are acting perfectly normal. It is their normal, not society's normal in terms of acceptable behavior. The response from mental health professionals has been to label these children with diagnoses such as attention-deficit/hyperactivity disorder (ADHD), reactive attachment disorder (RAD), bipolar disorder, oppositional defiant disorder (ODD), conduct disorder (CD), and other childhood mental health disorders.

These children are simply operating out of their right hemispheres, yet we have been parenting them from the left hemisphere. We have been giving them logic and expecting to modify their behaviors and we have been asking them to think through their "choices," both of which are left-hemisphere activities. We have neglected to address their deeper emotional states of fear. This is not the way the brain is designed. We cannot simply consciously "think away" our unconscious fears.

These mental health labels are indicative of children who are in a heightened state of fear, stress, and overwhelm. These children have experiences of not having their needs met, having been emotionally and/or physically hurt, having suffered significant relationship breaks, and/or intense medical experiences. **Simply, these are children who have experienced trauma.** They need to be loved in order to heal, not to have love removed from them through fear-based parenting techniques.

■

They need to be loved in order to heal, not have love removed from them through fear-based parenting techniques.

■

Reaching our children and parenting our children in a way that fosters strong relationships and teaches unconditional love will take operating from a new paradigm, an emotional paradigm that allows us to humanize our children again. It will require having the courage to set aside the behavior, digging deeper within ourselves to understand what it means to put love into action, and swimming upstream against what is culturally considered good parenting.

CHAPTER THREE

The Power of Love and Relationship

■

Humans are designed to be in relationship. We are designed to grow up in families and live in communities. What is considered the most severe punishment of an inmate in prison? Solitary confinement. This is because we are neurologically and biologically designed to be in relationship. Being alone for extended periods of time goes against our physiology.

Our children need connection in order to feel love, accepted, and safe. They cannot sufficiently create this on their own. They need to experience this first from their caregivers before they can give it to themselves. Children, especially babies, do not have the ability to "regulate" on their own.

A baby crying in a crib is communicating that he is in need of help. The baby is seeking regulation. The baby has slipped into a state of dysregulation, needing to be fed, rocked, cuddled, or have a diaper changed. The baby is incapable of shifting from this state of dysregulation to a state of regulation on his own. If the baby is not cared for, he goes into a hyper-aroused state, whereby the stress hormones excrete excessively until ultimately, the body will protect itself from creating internal damage by shutting down. The baby then stops crying and appears to have settled down.

Yet in actuality, the baby has not shifted back into a state of regulation. The baby has simply shifted from a state of active arousal to a state of passive arousal, still dysregulated at the internal level. He has been denied an interactive experience with his caregiver. He has missed the vital experience of being calmed and soothe, or regulated, by his caregiver.

This same concept is true for any child. When a child is acting out, it is a sign that the child has slipped into a state of dysregulation. If the child has not had enough past regulatory experiences of being soothed through the power of a loving relationship, the child's ability to self-regulate is insufficient to shift to a state of regulation on his own. Whether describing an infant or a 15-year-old child who is dysregulated, the role of the parent is always to join with the child in order to help the child regulate back to a state of calm arousal.

■

The role of the parent is always to join with the child in order to help the child regulate back to a state of calm arousal.

■

Science is showing that essential regulatory functions occur in the right hemisphere. The right hemisphere is responsible for the processing of positive and negative affective states, such as interest, excitement, and joy, along with pain, fear, and overwhelm. The right hemisphere controls the human stress response system and cortisol secretion as well as vital functions supporting survival. When a child's early experiences do not include predictability, quality care-giving, loving interactions, and safety, these functions of the right hemisphere are impaired and the ability to regulate is compromised.

When parenting a child with difficult behaviors, look into the child's past experiences and you will discover a history of disruption. In order to help a child get back on track, it takes connecting with the child at the emotional level. This connection happens in the right brain, so it is not the words that are important. It is the facial expression, tone and volume of voice, as well as the posture, tempo, and timing of movement. It is about learning to simply be present with your child and allowing the child the emotional space to process though his stress.

■

It is not what you say, but how you say it.

■

This is an interactive process between the parent and the child, and thus, it is imperative that the parent be in a state of regulation. If the caregiver is stressed out and dysregulated herself, her ability to create a state of regulation for her child is severely compromised. Have you ever been in a store and watched a stressed-out parent instructing her child to, "Calm down. Calm down, right now!"? The words are effective words; however, the delivery of the words is far more important to consider. It is not what you say, but how you say it.

Imagine having the opportunity to sit next to Gandhi, Jesus Christ, or Mother Teresa. How do you think you would feel simply sitting next to any one of these individuals who simply radiate love? Would your system automatically shift to a state of regulation? You undoubtedly would feel a sense of calm and peacefulness, even if words were not exchanged.

While this may be an extreme example, you do have the same ability to create this type of connection with your child. This is the power of love and relationship. This is "interactive regulation." Interactive regulation is the ability to easily regulate one's emotional state through interactions with others. As your child experiences these interactions with you and through you, he will gain experiential knowledge of what it feels like to be regulated. He will have experiences of going from a state of dysregulation and upset to a state of peace and calm.

As the child experiences this interactive regulation through your relationship with him, he then learns how to self-regulate, or as science is terming it, to "autoregulate." This is the ultimate gift we can give our child, to be able to self-regulate in times of stress, without others and without external measures.

You know what I am talking about when I say external measures-that cup of coffee you picked up before work today or the candy bar you downed at 3:00 this afternoon to keep you going. We all use external sources to help regulate us when we feel as if we cannot do it on our own. The ultimate goal is to teach our children to develop their innate internal capacity to self-regulate in order to keep them from seeking more severe external sources such as alcohol or drugs.

Childhood is the most opportune time to accomplish this goal. Science is showing that positive emotional experiences carve permanent pathways into a child's developing neurological system. Every interaction you have with your child is an opportunity to help your child regulate, make a positive emotional connection, and literally lay down neural networks that will enhance his brain's capacity to handle stress and overwhelm later in life. Conversely, research states that if a significant amount of a child's early emotional experiences is characterized by fear, then a negative and hopeless perspective becomes part of the child's personality framework.

It is important to realize these experiences influence a child far more than we once believed. In the past, it was believed that children who grow up with an abundance of experiences of distress, fear, separation, and rage simply develop bad behaviors and bad habits. We now know that it goes much deeper than this; they develop ingrained negative neurological pathways that control much of what they do.

The good news is that our brains are ever changing and ever creating new neuropathways. Neuroplasticity is the brain's ability to reorganize itself by forming new neural connections based on life experiences. Yet it is vital to the healing of our children that these new neuropathways are formed from emotional experiences, not intellectual or cognitive experiences.

These emotional experiences are not experiences that can be created in a therapist's office once a week for 50 minutes. These healing moments happen every day in our homes, 24 hours a day. It is in the moments when your child is most "raw" and the most dysregulated that you are being presented with an opportunity to create change and healing. It takes parenting from not just a new perspective but from an entirely new paradigm.

The *Beyond Consequences* parenting model presented in the next section of this book will give you examples of how to create these healing emotional experiences. It cannot be described as a technique and there are not hard and fast rules of "if this happens, then do this." Every situation with your child will be different and unique.

It takes living from a new paradigm of understanding how to put unconditional love into action in order to engage with your child. These experiences will be reaching your child in his right hemisphere which, as described above, is where you will be able to help him regulate back down to a state of calm. As a child is able to maintain this state of calm, he is then able to connect with his parent and develop a much healthier sense of self. This also enables him to form healthy and significant relationships in the future.

Addressing a child from the understanding that his behavior is reflective of his level of regulation will put you in alignment with the core issue driving your child's behavior. By helping him regulate through his relationship with you, he will be developing his ability to regulate on his own. The ability to self-regulate during times of stress and overwhelm will afford him the ability to stay within behavioral boundaries and the negative behaviors will dissipate. He will truly be able to make good choices because he will be able to access his left brain – his thinking, logical, and rational brain.

As you read through the series of questions and answers that follow, describing how to put love into action, recognize that much of what you read will be the opposite of what you have always been taught and read in most parenting books. It will take courage to trust in the power of love and relationship rather than the power of control and punishment. The reality is that no one likes to be controlled, especially children who have experienced relational trauma. Thus, the basic premise of this approach is flawed from the start.

■

The reality is that no one likes to be controlled, especially children who have experienced relationship trauma.

■

Becoming a *Beyond Consequences* parent will mean you:
1. Asking the right question *("What is driving my child's behavior?")*
2. Recognizing that we are in a new era with scientific evidence of how our child's brain operates
3. Most importantly, removing the fear you have used in the past.

Simply put, it will take daring to love your child in a whole new way!

PART TWO

Questions and Answers

Introduction to the Beyond Consequences Parenting Paradigm

Q: *I need a quick way to explain to my parents what is meant by "Parenting Beyond Consequences." They don't seem to understand the way I'm parenting and are quite critical of me. They aren't interested in the neuroscience or the brain research. They are simply coming from the old school of the basics, so any help you have would be appreciated!*

A: *Beyond Consequences* can be a difficult concept to understand and to "wrap your brain around" when you have been living in a more traditional mindset for years, even generations. Love is about meeting people where they are and respecting their perspectives. Understanding that your parents are looking through the lens of the "old school" is the first place to start. From such a point of reference, this model is sometimes interpreted as if you are coddling or babying your child. The following explanation is written in more general terms in order to help a grandparent, relative, or anyone, begin to make a shift. Remember to be patient; you are shifting an entire paradigm for living.

Children need unconditional love and unconditional acceptance from their parents; we all know this and believe this. However, do we ever stop to consider how so many of the traditional parenting techniques accepted in our culture work contrary to this primal goal? Traditional parenting techniques that involve consequences, controlling directives, and punishment are fear-based and fear-driven. They have the ability to undermine the parent-child relationship and because they are tied to behavior, children easily interpret these actions to mean, "If I'm not good, I am not lovable." Thus, children often build a subconscious foundation that says that love and approval is based on performance.

> ■
> *Remember to be patient; you are shifting an entire paradigm for living.*
> ■

Parenting from a love-based paradigm means going beyond our children's behavior and beyond consequences to first see that negative behavior is a form of communication and that negative behavior is a response to stress. If we see the kicking and screaming child as one who is having difficulty regulating due to an overflow of feelings, we can learn to stay present with the child in order to help him modulate these feelings and thus, help him build his emotional regulatory system. A child kicking and screaming or in a rage is a child who has been "emotionally hijacked." Emotions are not logical or rational; this hitting and kicking is the body's natural fear reaction in hyperdrive.

Allowing a child emotional space to safely dissipate this energy will then allow him to calm down. As we provide reassurance, unconditional love, and emotional presence for our children, the need to kick and scream will disappear. Many times our children kick and scream simply because they do not feel that they are being listened to nor do they feel as if they have been heard. Staying present and reassuring a child that you really are listening to him, can be enough to help him begin to regulate. The life lesson that kicking and screaming is inappropriate does indeed need to be reinforced. But, this life lesson can only happen once the child is fully regulated (when the child is calm) and his cognitive thinking is intact. This is also the time to present alternatives to kicking and screaming. This is a way of teaching our children instead of punishing them. **The definition of discipline is to teach.**

The more we can stay focused on the relationship with our child and strengthening this relationship instead of controlling it through consequences, the more we will be helping our child learn to work through his stress appropriately. Below are four pointers to help you stay in a loving and emotionally open place for your children:

1. Just Be Happy! – But I'm not! Did anyone ever tell you, "Just think happy thoughts and it will be okay."? Did it really work? Probably not. Emotions do not simply disappear. If feelings are not released and acknowledged, they are stored and become part of our physical make-up. Research has convincingly shown that being able to express feelings like anger and grief can improve survival rates in cancer patients. With our children, feelings that become stored and "stuffed" become activators for negative behaviors.

2. ALL Feelings are Good Feelings – As parents, it is important for us to understand the necessity of emotional expression, both in teaching it to our children and in modeling it to our children. Blocked feelings can inhibit growth, learning, and the building of a trusting relationship between the parent and child. The first step to take is to recognize that ALL emotions are healthy. In our culture, feelings such as joy, peace, and courage are seen as good feelings, yet feelings such as sad, mad, and scared are seen as bad feelings. Let's rethink this to understand that it is not the feeling itself that creates negativity; it is the lack of expression of the feeling that creates negativity. And in children, this negativity is often expressed through poor behaviors.

3. Getting to the Core of the Behavior – When children are acting out and being defiant, we need to begin to understand that their behaviors are simply a communication of an emotional state that is driving these behaviors. If we simply address the behavior, we miss the opportunity to help children express and understand themselves from a deeper level. Start by modeling basic feeling words for your child. Keep it simple and teach the five basic feeling words: sad, mad, bad, scared, and happy. Even the youngest of children can learn to say, "I'm mad!" When the toddler is throwing his toys or the teenager is throwing his backpack across the room, encourage him at that moment to get to the core of the behavior through emotional expression. Remember . . . it really isn't about the toys or the backpack; and they really do know better than to act out with the negative behaviors.

4. Responding vs. Reacting – So the next time your child becomes defiant, talks back, or is simply "ugly" to you, work to be in a place that lets you not react to the behavior, but respond to your child. Respond to your child in an open way – open to meeting him in his heart and helping him understand the overload of feelings that are driving the behaviors. He does not need a consequence or another parental directive at that moment; he just needs you to be present with him. As your children learn to respond to you through the parent-child relationship, they will not have the need to communicate through negative behaviors anymore. You will both have more energy for each other, building a relationship that will last a lifetime.

Q: *I understand that my daughter has a difficult time regulating, but if I'm not giving consequences, then does she think that her behavior is okay? I am struggling because it is not acceptable to be disrespectful to me. Her behavior is so appalling! I understand how reacting can be disempowering, but what can I do that is empowering in that moment that sends the right message to her?*

A: If we go back to the understanding that negative behavior comes from an unconscious place (see Chapter 1, *Beyond Consequences, Logic, and Control, Volume 1*), we can begin to see that disrespect is about something much deeper. This level of disrespect typically begins with early life experiences when a child's needs are not met. Your daughter is simply acting out of the model that was imprinted within her system.

These are the patterns that bind us. If you try to change the behavior in her moment of distress, you will find yourself frustrated at the lack of change. This is because we cannot learn when we are stressed out. Stress inhibits our cognitive thinking. So the life lesson of being respectful, even when angry, needs to come when your daughter is calm and regulated. Work to calm her nervous system and her emotional state. Really listen to her. Many times children (and we as adults) become disrespectful, rude, and/or loud because we do not feel like we are being heard.

Connect with her disrespect instead of trying to shut it down. When you truly listen to what is behind the disrespect, you will find the depth of overwhelm and fear your daughter is experiencing and trying to express.

Saying something like, "Sweetheart, when you speak disrespectfully, that only tells me that you're hurting inside. It also tells me that you might be feeling disrespected." Join her instead of correcting her.

Your daughter needs you to help her connect with her overwhelm; she cannot do it on her own. She is reacting to you because it is too big and overwhelming for her system. The message you will be sending back to her at that very moment is one of respect, compassion, and love. You will be giving her the message that strengthening your relationship with her is your primary goal—that she is more important to you than anything else on this planet.

Certainly the long-term goal is to teach our children to be respectful to their parents and that we should all live a life of obedience. Yet when this lesson is given in the heat of the moment, defensive, disrespectful, and defiant feedback loops are created. The most important point is when we stay focused solely on the behavior, the real consequence is that relationships are broken and the relationship's focus becomes control and power, not love and connection.

> ■
> *The real consequence is that the relationship's focus becomes control and power, not love and connection.*
> ■

So, an hour later, that evening, or sometime when you both are better connected, talk to her about the disrespect and discuss options and ways to handle it differently the next time. Express your reactions to her behavior and how it makes you feel. Perhaps relate a story of your own experience from your past that would connect with her. All of this will help her learn how to connect with herself when she begins to get stressed out and dysregulated. This will empower her to come to you for help in a loving and respectful way and it will empower her to develop her own regulatory ability to handle stressful situations as an adult.

Parenting out of this love-based approach is hard work. In most cases, it would be much easier to give out a consequence and be done with it. Yet, when we truly understand that negative behavior does not come from a cognitive, rational place, we realize that giving consequences is actually quite irrational and illogical. This book is not designed to help you simply learn a new parenting technique. Rather, this book is about learning an entirely new paradigm. It is a paradigm that you live out of and a paradigm in which your perspective of the world is forever changed. It is a perspective whose foundation is based in love and in the understanding that power does not come from control, but through loving, respectful, and caring influence.

Q: *Using the Beyond Consequences approach feels like the child is getting lots of positive attention for negative behaviors and I am having a hard time with this idea. What about the idea that where we focus our attention is what we get more of? I love my children unconditionally, but I still want them to learn how to behave because the world is not going to love them unconditionally.*

A: The *Beyond Consequences* approach is often challenging for parents and professionals who have been ingrained in the behavioral approach and in the area of behavioral modification. If you have been focused solely on the behavior and the outcome of a child's actions, it can be difficult, if not impossible at first, to look beyond this.

However, it is like comparing apples to oranges. *Beyond Consequences* addresses the child's stress state, not the child's behavior. Making this shift in our focus is imperative to understanding how to respond to our children.

Instead of seeing that children act out because they want attention, it takes seeing that children act out because they need attention. The words **want** and **need** have two distinct meanings. The word "want" means to wish for or to desire, while the word "need" means to require.

Love is a requirement for children (and adults). Our children need our attention as part of their growing process. If we have been unable to attend to their needs or to connect with them in relationship to the fullest extent possible (due to life stressors), the only way for them to get the love they need is to act out through negative behaviors.

Often times, parents have reacted to this behavior by giving them consequences or taking away privileges. In doing so, parents are giving them "attention." Unfortunately, this type of attention is negative. So, the child is asking for love and the parent responds by giving the child negative attention. This negativity then influences how a child defines love.

It is important to realize that for children, any form of concentrated attention, whether positive or negative, is interpreted as love. Ironically, not wanting to give our children attention for negative behaviors has essentially been teaching them negative definitions of love.

The result is that love becomes rejection. Love becomes abandonment. Love becomes pain. And if we ignore the child's behaviors, love becomes indifference. Love becomes "you don't matter to me."

Have you ever wondered why your best friend or colleague continues to cycle through relationships where she chooses the same type of person? She continues to date men who reject her or who diminish her? You find yourself saying, "He's just like the last guy she dated!" Our childhood relationships define our understanding and perception of love. If, at a subconscious level, our mind believes that love is rejection, we then seek out relationships that fit this definition. While we may hold a different belief about love at a conscious level, our subconscious is what drives our behaviors 85% of the time.

It is our responsibility as parents to give our children the true definition of love. Love is patience. Love is kindness. Love is unconditional acceptance. Love is validation. Love is understanding. Love is time together. Love is tolerance. Love is security. Love is listening. Love is commitment. Love is approval. Love is nurturing. Love is being instead of doing. Love is flexibility.

You are right that the world is not going to love your child unconditionally; however, by creating a secure base of support and unconditional love from you, your child will be equipped to go out into the world, knowing that he is still loved and accepted. From this place, he will have the ability and the resources to behave in socially appropriate ways.

Remember, *Beyond Consequences* does not totally ignore behavior, but recognizes that parents need to teach the child when the child is regulated and can learn what is acceptable. In moments of dysregulation, the child can not learn. Stress causes confused and distorted thinking. What we need to teach is how to regulate in the midst of stress. Joining our child in his dysregulation is how we help equip our child to develop his own regulatory system. This will empower and equip your child to grow up and be a regulated and loving adult in a world that is often times dysregulated and fearful.

Parenting is about putting love into action. In order to put this love into action, it takes loving our children beyond their behaviors. It takes going beyond consequences, logic, and control to meet our children's needs.

Q: *What? I can't do this! If I don't use consequences, then my house will be chaos!*

A: A house without boundaries would be a house in chaos; however, consequences are different from boundaries. Children absolutely need boundaries in order to establish limits and predictability. Boundaries create safety and security for children.

The *Beyond Consequences* model understands that when children step outside of these boundaries, it is because they are in a state of dysregulation and are driven from an unconscious place of fear and overwhelm. It is fear that has moved them outside of the boundaries.

Traditional parenting methods use fear to move the child back into boundaries. Yet, how logical is it to use fear and control to "teach" a child who is already scared and overwhelmed? This does nothing to help a child learn how to stay in a place of love and it teaches a child to grow up to be controlling and authoritative. More importantly, it drives a wedge in the relationship between the parent and the child. Children learn to be obedient out of fear, not love.

We want our children to wake up everyday and subconsciously say, "I want to please my parents and be obedient because I respect them. I want to do what they ask simply because I love them." Traditional models put children in a place to be obedient out of fear, not out of loving respect and reverence.

Consequences are reactive. They are a negative form of concentrated attention tied to a negative behavior. In mathematics, multiplying a negative number times a negative equals a positive number. However, in parenting, addressing a negative with a negative only creates more negativity and weakens the parent-child relationship.

Thus, when a child moves outside of the boundaries, the *Beyond Consequences* model works to continue loving this child in order to reconnect the child in relationship with the parent. This is the definition of unconditional love-love with no conditions-love not based on how we act, what we do, or how we behave.

It is the parent's responsibility to join the child in his distress and help him shift back into the boundaries through love, understanding, and acceptance. In doing so, the parent is helping to regulate the child, which will build the child's own ability to regulate.

The graphic examples below help illustrate this concept. In Figure A, the dashed line represents the boundary established by the parents for the child. The child is within the boundaries (the thick dashed line) and is in an emotional state of love. When children are in a state of love, they act loving and respectful. Additionally, this loving behavior is comfortable for parents and thus, his parents are loving and accepting towards him. It is easy to love an obedient child.

In Figure B, the child has shifted from a state of love to a state of fear. The child has been unable to regulate the level of stress in his life. Something in this child's life has overwhelmed him to the point he can not stay within the boundaries (not won't, but *can't*).

Figure A   Figure B

In Figure C, the parent is frustrated and having a difficult time getting the child back into a place of obedience. The child is becoming more dysregulated and fearful of the parent. Sometimes the child is able to make the shift back into a place of obedience as seen in Figure D. It was fear that moved the child back, not love. The child continues to be upset and resentful of the parent. Both parent and child are upset with one another and the relationship is clearly strained.

Figure C   Figure D

Now let us look at the *Beyond Consequences* love-based approach to boundaries. The parent focuses on maintaining and strengthening the parent-child relationship, not correcting the behaviors at the moment.

Figure E   Figure F

The parent recognizes that the child is in an emotional state of fear (You can also use the words overwhelm and pain if you are having a hard time seeing the fear in your child). In this state of fear, the child has difficulty accessing his cognitive brain and is not thinking logically or rationally. Addressing the child from a behavioral standpoint, giving the child logical directives and expecting the child to change his behavior is irrational. The *Beyond Consequences* parent recognizes that the child needs assistance getting regulated in order to be able to process his act of defiance. The parent works to regulate herself, joins the child, and then helps to move the child back into the boundaries-back into a state of love.

The relationship is intact and the child's stress state has been calmed. Through the parent's unconditional love, acceptance, and understanding, the child develops a deeper relationship with his parent. Later, when both are calm, the parent is able to talk to the child and discuss ways to stay regulated next time, instead of being disobedient and stepping outside the boundaries. The parent has created the opportunity to express her own frustration and sadness that developed from the child's negative behavior.

The child is in a calmer state, which opens him up to this emotional exchange and prepares him to stay more regulated in the future. As these love-based interactions are repeated over and over, the child develops a larger capacity for stress; his regulatory system expands and develops in order to appropriately handle stressful situations in the future while staying inside the boundaries. The child is being empowered to make his own decisions and choices based on his internal sense of right and wrong, not making choices based off of, "What is going to happen to me if I get caught?"

Q: *I just don't see the fear. I mean, what's so scary about cleaning your room or making your bed? Isn't my child just being lazy?*

A: As suggested in the previous answer, it can be helpful to use the word "overwhelm" instead of fear. As parents, we need to work to see how these tasks can be overwhelming to our children. First, let us look at an example in our own lives. Sometimes when you walk into your office or your laundry room, do you get overwhelmed with the idea of handling all the work you see in front of you? It just looks like too much. As adults, we have developed ways to reduce this stress. It may be looking at the pile of laundry and saying, "Okay, I'm going to just do the jeans and leave everything else in the pile." We have learned how to take an overwhelming task and break it down into manageable parts.

For a child who is asked to clean his room, it can be as overwhelming as walking through New Orleans after Hurricane Katrina and wondering,

"Where do we begin?"

The definition of discipline is "to teach." The child who is appearing lazy or defiant by not cleaning his room is a child who needs his parent's help in breaking down the chore at hand. Instead of fighting the situation and jumping into a control battle, it would be more productive to the development of the relationship to simply join the child and offer your help. The parent might say, "Son, it looks like cleaning your room is a bit overwhelming. What if we do it together?" The parent then shows and teaches the child how to break down a daunting task into parts that become manageable.

Many times the parent's fear response to this example is, "If I do if for him now, how is he ever going to learn to do it himself?" or "If I do it for him this time, he will want me to do it every time." To answer this, we must realize that many children are functioning at a level far below their chronological age. Due to interruptions in their development caused by traumatic experiences, they may be years behind in their functioning. An eight year-old may actually be more like a three-year-old. We would not expect a three-year-old to be able to make his bed by himself or clean up his room by himself. At this three-year-old age, the parent would assist the child in this task in order to teach him. Meeting a child at his emotional age will allow the child to experience life at a level that is manageable and challenging enough, while not completely overpowering his regulatory system.

This is also an opportunity to join your child in relationship. We become so focused on outcomes that we totally miss the process and the joy of parenting. Yes, "joy of parenting." Parenting is supposed to be filled with joy and is supposed to be pleasurable. Seek to create a space of love within you so your child can find the security and safety he needs in order to return to the happy and joyful child he is designed to be.

Children are created in a spirit of love. They are designed to be happy and joyful, not lazy and disobedient. We must trust that children are not inherently lazy. Believing that a child is inherently lazy is a false belief that we have developed in our society. It is when we slip into overwhelm that we remove ourselves from our reality in order to attempt to regain a sense of balance. It is when we are in this state of dysregulation that we exhibit laziness. It is a natural coping mechanism we use in order to settle our nervous system and reduce our internal state of discomfort.

Back to the example of your overflowing laundry room or office; how would you feel if your spouse or friend came in and started giving you orders to clean it up or else? Or how would you feel if this person, instead, came in and noticed how overwhelmed you were and said to you, "This looks like a big task, how about I help you with it?" Which one would help you calm down and more importantly, which one would make you feel special, loved, and important?

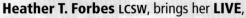

Q: *If a child is not taught through consequences, how will he ever learn to live in a world filled with consequences?*

A: When you are teaching your children to drive a car, do you teach them how to get into an accident so they are prepared for one in the future? Of course not! Instead, we teach our children how to be defensive drivers in order to prevent and be free of accidents.

This analogy demonstrates the idea of teaching our children consequences because we live in a world filled with consequences. Think about this important concept: **Instead of teaching our children how to suffer consequences, we need to teach them how to stay regulated in order to avoid consequences.** The first is reactive parenting. The second is proactive parenting.

Reactive parenting is characterized by consequences and control that is focused solely on behavior in order to have compliant children who do as they are told. Proactive parenting is teaching our children how to stay regulated during stressful times in order to develop their own internal control mechanisms. Which paradigm do you want to embrace?

Reactive parenting leaves children living in a fear-based world, where they make decisions and choices based on the consequences of their actions, rather than making decisions based on how their choices can help or benefit those around them. Decisions are made based on "What will happen to me if I do this?" How limiting this is for our children!

Proactive parenting allows children to live within a much more open internal framework of love and acceptance, giving them the space and freedom to make decisions based on their own internal moral compass.

Parenting beyond consequences, logic, and control helps give our children the practice during childhood to develop their own internal controls. This prepares them to be able to function at a higher level of consciousness when they are adults. It gives them the ability to live beyond the fear of consequences. Living in fear limits us and creates unnecessary barriers.

The dominant belief in our culture is that we need external measures in order to keep us living an ethical and moral life. The deeper truth is that we have the ability to develop all of this within ourselves through adopting core values and through our ability to connect with others in loving and respectful relationships.

Core values that are given the space to have a voice determine our behavior. Loving relationships create desire and internal motivation to live by these values. When we are connected with others in safe relationships, we have empathy and are in touch with our feelings. We are able to live far beyond our primal needs whereby we can tap into the deeper levels within us that distinguish us from all other creatures on this planet.

Consequences from parents teach fear and rejection. This fear and rejection then transcends to teaching the child self-rejection. "If my parents don't love me, then I must not be worthy. I must not deserve love." Self-acceptance, self-validation, and self-worth are absent or limited within the child's framework.

Yet, these are qualities that we want to instill in our children based on who they are, not on what they do or how they act. Our children need to know they are intrinsically valuable, worthy, and deserving of unconditional love. When these qualities make up the blueprint of their personality and their inner selves, they do not need external consequences to keep them within the parameters of society. They develop much stronger boundaries and a powerful sense of right and wrong from within themselves.

We figure out very early in life that the external consequences used to enforce boundaries only apply to you if you get caught. It is a tragedy to think about how much time and energy is spent making sure we do not get caught in order to avoid consequences. We are all guilty of speeding down the street and then hitting the brakes when we see a police car. What would it take to shift your thinking to that of, "I'm going to go the speed limit in order to be safe for myself and for those around me," instead of "I'm going to go the speed limit because I can't afford a ticket or for my insurance rates increase"?

It is self-love that breeds respect for ourselves and for others. Self-love and self-respect keep us in a place of integrity and keep us moving forward in our lives. Self-motivation, self-discipline, and self-awareness are all by-products of this love for self. These internal controls, not consequences created by parents or society, are the original design to keep us on the straight and narrow path.

Love allows us to swim in the deep end, free to live a fulfilling life and free to think beyond consequences in order to dream big and live in peace, abundance, and happiness.

We need to stop living our lives in a pool of fear. It keeps us treading water in the shallow end, constricted and limited. Love allows us to swim in the deep end, free to live a fulfilling life and free to think beyond consequences in order to dream big and live in peace, abundance, and happiness. Love allows us to develop the ability to self-regulate in times of stress in order to stay calm enough to make the right decisions and choices.

Through our parenting, we have the ability to give our children the gift of self-regulation so they may live productive, happy, and abundant lives in a world filled with consequences.

Q: *When does the child learn that not everyone is going to love them through a fit of rage if they are not taught consequences of actions? I believe children kicking and screaming without interventions will still be kicking and screaming as teenagers.*

A: To better understand why we need to go beyond this behavior and beyond giving consequences, we need to first truly understand that negative behavior is a form of communication and that negative behavior is a response to stress. Additionally, if we view the kicking and screaming as a child who is having difficulty regulating, we can learn to stay present with the child in order to help build his regulatory system (and yes, safety is always first). A child kicking and screaming or in a rage, is a child who has been "emotionally hijacked."

Emotions are not logical or rational. For a child in a deep state of dysregulation, this hitting and kicking is the body's natural fear reaction. This fear response of "fighting for their lives" has been built up at the body level within many of our children. Peter Levine, in his *Healing Trauma* audio series, says it best: "It is as though our survival energies are all dressed up with no place to go."

Allowing a child the emotional space to safely dissipate this energy will then allow him the emotional space to calm down. As we provide reassurance, unconditional love, and emotional presence for our children, the need to kick and scream will disappear. Additionally, many times our children kick and scream simply because they do not feel as if they are being listened to nor do they feel as if they have been heard. Staying present and reassuring a child that you really are listening to him can be enough to help him begin to regulate.

The life lesson does indeed need to be continually reinforced: that kicking and screaming is inappropriate. But, this life lesson can only happen once the brain is fully regulated and the thinking part of the brain is engaged (See *Beyond Consequences, Logic, and Control, Volume 2* for a discussion of the brain). Thus, when the child is calm and his cognitive thinking is intact, the life lesson can be given along with alternatives to kicking and screaming. This is a way of teaching our children instead of punishing them . . . the definition of discipline is to teach.

As children are helped into a regulated state, they build their window of stress tolerance; they build their ability to stay regulated during times of stress. As this window of stress tolerance is increased, they become equipped as teenagers and young adults to stay regulated instead of becoming dysregulated and reactive. When relationships in the family are based in love rather than fear, they are strong enough to handle the trials of being a teenager. Family members are open to listening and staying connected during life's most difficult moments, thus eliminating the need for raging teenagers.

Q: *I have to say that in the two weeks we have been using the techniques in the book, my son has gone from occasional and minor non-compliance to a constant source of rude talking, anger, misbehavior and general disruption. As of yesterday we are trying to forget everything we learned in an effort to recover from this catastrophic experiment. I guess it doesn't work for everyone.*

A: It can be frustrating and disheartening to see negativity in a home intensify when trying to make positive changes. Implementing a new technique in the home can create disruption because you have now become different from what your child is accustomed to expecting. The *Beyond Consequences* paradigm is an absolute 180 degree shift from traditional methods. Yet, an increase in negative behavior can actually be seen as a step in the right direction for families beginning their journey down the *Beyond Consequences* healing road.

We traditionally use behaviors as a gauge to determine whether our child is "good" or "bad." We are a behaviorally based society, where the behavior determines either success or failure. Unfortunately with this approach, we deny the process and only focus on the end result. With sensitive children (i.e., children acting out with defiant and severe behaviors), losing our focus on the process creates fear within us as parents. If we only see rude talking, anger, and misbehavior, then all we see is failure. In this fear, we revert back to doing the same parenting we have always done, over and over again. Yet in this fear-driven distortion, we actually expect a different outcome.

I want to encourage you to see that the change in behavior, albeit an increase in negative behavior, is actually a sign of an improved process. This child is expressing more of himself and sharing his pain and fear with you. Children have to be taught how to express themselves in positive ways, but in the meantime, we have to accept this as all they know. Attitudes and "sassiness" are simply a communication of a deeper fear-based issue.

Now be honest with yourself when answering this question: When you've been stressed out, felt like you are not being heard, or felt completely overwhelmed, did you ever react to those closest to you in a disrespectful, angry, or inappropriate way? I am thinking your answer is "yes." We act like this when we have no other means of getting someone to connect with us and connect with our needs.

I believe that by implementing the *Beyond Consequences* paradigm in your home, you have actually created more safety and more emotional space for your child to move out of a hypo-aroused state (inwardly shut-down state) into a hyper-aroused state (outwardly, angry state). By increasing the level of safety, removing the threat of punishment, and responding instead of reacting, you have created space for this child to express himself. What a victory! But it is only a victory if you stay focused on the process. It is vital to accept that the process may be "ugly" and "uncomfortable" and yes, "disrespectful" (as seen from the traditional model). Yet, if we truly understand that all negative behavior arises from an unconscious state, it should not be difficult to accept this.

Meeting our children exactly where they are is the only way to move them forward to exactly where we think they should be.

I remember when my own daughter made this shift from hypo-aroused to hyper-aroused. I found myself actually celebrating that she was having tantrums! Finally, she was venturing out of her shell and getting in touch with her fear. This was my opportunity to reach her and to connect with her in order to show her what a safe relationship with a mother could be like.

■
Love works
for everyone.
■

Creating emotional safety and space for emotional expression is scary and it takes courage. Love works for everyone. It is simply a matter of focusing on the relationship and focusing on the process. In doing so, the ONLY possible outcome to follow will be "good behavior."

Q: *A lot of your information talks about working through past trauma. What if I have very little information about my child's past experiences? My step-daughter lived with my husband's ex-wife prior to coming to live with us at five years old and experienced significant neglect in her home.*

A: While you may not have the specifics of your daughter's early life experiences, the main ingredient missing in her past is a safe and strong relationship with a primary attachment figure. This primary early relationship directly influences how the brain develops.

Dr. Bruce Perry, an expert in the field of trauma, was asked in an interview, "How do relationships affect the way the brain develops?" His response:

"Human beings are, at our core, relational creatures. We are designed to live, work, play and grow in groups. The very nature of humanity arises from relationships. You learn language, you learn social language, you learn appropriate emotional regulation, and essentially everything that's important about life as a human being you learn in the context of relationships. And the very substance of a successful individual is bathed in a whole host of relationships with people in that person's life. When there are positive relationships, there literally are physiological changes in the person's brain and in their body that make them more physically, emotionally and socially at risk." *(Santa Barbara Graduate Institute-Producer. 2004. Trauma, Brain and Relationship [Documentary].)*

So what this means for your daughter is that she needs you to provide her with the chance to recover what was missing in the past. The details of her trauma could be helpful in some situations, but they are not critical.

Every interaction you have with her is a chance to repattern her neurological system. Your child has a high degree of plasticity. Plasticity is the lifelong ability of the brain to reorganize neural pathways based on new experiences. **Just as traumatic experiences have the ability to change the brain, nurturing experiences also have the ability to change the brain.**

Environment plays a key role in influencing plasticity. Stay attuned to your own regulation and your mood during the course of each day and what type of environment you are creating for your child. It is not so much *what* you say, as it is *how* you say it. Ask yourself these questions when interacting with your child:

(1) "Is this a nurturing and authentic response?"
(2) "Is the tone of my voice safe?"
(3) "What is the position of my body; is it creating more threat?"
(4) "Is the timing of my response allowing my child enough emotional space to process her internal signals?"
(5) "Am I taking my child's behavior personally or am I working to understand her behavior from her perspective?"

As you practice and stay in a place of awareness, parenting in the *Beyond Consequences* model will become more automatic. It is hard work at first, but your ability to change your child's brain for life is the greatest calling ever to be bestowed upon anyone.

Q: *Do these theories and concepts apply to children who have not suffered a trauma? Is fear always the basis of negative behaviors?*

A: Yes, the *Beyond Consequences* approach works for all children. When a child is acting out, he has shifted from a state of regulation (love) to a state of dysregulation (fear). He is outside of his window of stress tolerance and needs connection to help him shift back into balance. When children misbehave, there is a break in the attachment relationship. The child needs the parent to help him reconnect.

Unfortunately, the traditional response has been to issue consequences at times of misbehavior. This type of reactive response only serves to drive a wedge into this parent/child relationship.

Our role as parents and caretakers is to meet our children's needs. Children are not born with the ability to verbally express their needs, so they use the only tools they have – their behaviors. You would not expect a newborn baby to say, "Mom, I'm hungry." Crazy, right? But we expect children, even young toddlers, to inherently be able to express their needs appropriately. We then react to behaviors instead of respond to them from a place of love and understanding.

The more you can stay focused on the relationship and understand that a child's acting out behaviors are a communication of an unmet need, no matter their history, the more you will be able to strengthen your relationship with him. The stronger your relationship with your child, the more effective you will be as a parent. Effective parenting does not come through consequences, logic, and control. It comes through loving influence and connected relationships.

Q: *I am having a debate: some people think that the "Beyond Consequences Model" only works well with adopted children and may not work with others. I think you should be able to use it all the time.*

A: You are absolutely on target. The *Beyond Consequences* model works with all children. Should we not raise our children with love instead of fear? Traditional parenting works simply because typical children have a sufficient regulatory system. And thus, just about *any* parenting will work.

I have taught this model of parenting to parents who did not have adopted children – just parents dealing with some minor disruptive behaviors. It has helped families grow closer and develop more trusting relationships between the parents and the children. So, you are right on . . . love works for all children.

Dysregulation

Q: *I was recently given your book, "Beyond Consequences, Logic, and Control," by a friend of mine. My son has always been difficult to handle, even as a toddler (he is now 10 years old). You use the term "attachment-challenged" in your title and you make reference to the term "reactive attachment disorder" in your book as well. Could you explain these terms to me?*

■

Love works for all children.

■

A: In essence, I am hearing you ask, "What is attachment?" If we start in the dictionary, Webster defines attachment as "a feeling that binds one to a person, thing, cause, ideal, or the like." Interesting that they define it as a "feeling."

If we look at how the mental health field describes attachment, we can turn to the diagnosis of "reactive attachment disorder" or RAD. The Diagnostic and Statistical Manual of Mental Disorders (DMS-IV-TR) states, "the essential feature of Reactive Attachment Disorder is markedly disturbed and developmentally inappropriate social relatedness . . ." *(American Psychiatric Association. 2000. Diagnostic and statistical manual of mental disorders - 4th edition-text revision. Washington, DC: Author.)*

If we look at the work of John Bowlby, considered to be the "Father of Attachment Theory," we see another definition. In his book, *A Secure Base,* Bowlby's foundational view of attachment behavior is that of protection and safety. *(Bowlby, J. 1988. A Secure Base. London: Routledge)*

While all of these definitions are helpful in defining and understanding attachment, they still do not explain why children become so disruptive, violent, or disrespectful. If attachment is about being social, seeking relationships, and needing connection in order to feel safe, then would it not be rational for a child to seek his parent's help and love when he is upset or dysregulated?

So the question now becomes, "What interferes with attachment?" That is the question we need to be asking when our child is exhibiting negative behaviors. "What is interfering with my child's ability to seek attachment and connection with me?"

The answer is stress, fear, and overwhelm. It is in times of heightened stress that we cannot connect, cannot "attach." Think about a time when you became really stressed out and someone came up to comfort you. You reacted by saying, "No, just leave me alone." Stress has an amazing impact on our ability to stay in relationships.

Now we have some "real-life" application to this word "attachment".

When our children are misbehaving, they are stressed out. As parents, our role is not to force attachment because forcing attachment only creates more stress. Our role is to remove the stress or at least, lessen the stress.

Many times it can be as simple as identifying the stress and saying to our children, "You know, today is a hard day with Christmas just around the corner, final exams are in a few days, and plans for traveling over the holiday break are in full force. We're all stressed out right now." Simply identifying the stress can actually help calm the stress.

As you stay focused, not on attachment, but on the level of stress in the relationship, you will ultimately find that "feeling" of attachment that Webster defines. **You will be creating an environment where instinctual attachment behavior moves your children toward you, instead of away from you.**

Q: *I am wondering if you think it is helpful to educate children about their mental health diagnosis (such as ADHD or RAD). Should we teach them about how their difficulties stem from insecure attachments? If so, do you have any guidelines for how to share this with children?*

A: Yes, I absolutely think we should educate our children about their histories and how this has affected their neurological systems. It can be one of the most empowering ways to help children in their own healing process. Too many times we give our children a diagnosis, but then they use it in a self-limiting way. I can vividly remember a child I was working with in a school say to me, "I can't do that. I have ADHD." We need to be sure to help children understand why they react so easily and how to start making their lives different.

We can teach our children how to identify what overwhelms them and then they can begin to regulate their own environments. We need to teach them positive vocabulary words like "overwhelm," "regulated," "dysregulated," and "stress." Using these words, instead of self-limiting words and phrases such as, "I can't do it," or "I don't like doing that" keeps children from feeling as if they are not good enough or that something is wrong with them.

Give children their story. They need to know what happened to them in order to create more understanding and acceptance of who they are. This helps prevent children from going to a place of self-rejection. Even if you do not have specific details of their history, you can use words such as, "When you were a baby, you didn't have someone come help you in your crib like you needed to. When babies don't have the kind of love and nurturing they need, their systems don't know what to do with all the fear and sadness." Explain that because of this, their nervous systems become easily overwhelmed when they are under stress.

Yet, we do not want to stop here. We want to always work to empower our children to first have an understanding, but more importantly to take action to make their lives different. No matter what level of trauma they experienced in the past, they always have the ability to work towards healing. Shifting from a place of brokenness and darkness to a place of wholeness and light is always possible!

Empower your children to identify what events or activities create dysregulation for them. Help them learn how to monitor and modulate their environments. My daughter, at 13-years-old, was a master at this for herself. She decided not to attend a party with several other girls because, as she stated, "that would just be too overwhelming for me." When working on her homework, she would know exactly when to take a break, declaring to me, "I just need a break from this. It's too much right now." *Admittedly, I was the one still pushing her to just get one more math problem done!*

> **■**
> *We want to always work to empower our children to first have an understanding, but more importantly to take action to make their lives different.*
> **■**

Sir Francis Bacon said it best: "Knowledge is power." **The power to change, the power to heal, and the power to create a better life begins with knowledge and understanding.** Include your children in the learning process so they have an understanding of why they are "different" or have difficulties. This will move them to be a victor, not a victim.

Q: *Frequently, when our son visits someone else's home (grandparents, aunts, friends, etc.) without us, he comes back home dysregulated and out of control. Prior to these visits, he is doing well at home and they tell us that he was good with them. How can we help stop this cycle?*

A: The separation from you is too much for your son's regulatory system. It is putting him outside his window of stress tolerance. The positive piece here is that your son has developed the ability to stay regulated during his time away from you, hence the reports that he is behaving well during the visits. When he gets home, however, his system has been overly challenged and he simply cannot stay regulated.

The analogy that comes to mind is that of eating a chocolate bar. When you eat it, you get the rush of sugar, a burst of energy and you are feeling good. Then, all of a sudden, your blood sugar drops and you crash. This is what is happening to your son. He has to work incredibly hard to stay regulated when he is away from you, so when he gets home his system crashes.

In order to help ease the stress while he is away, here are a few suggestions. The best option to start would be to not leave him alone while visiting. Is there a way to stay with him during the visits? Your presence would give him the ability to be in a different environment and stay regulated. After a few visits with you there, you could begin to leave him for short stays and gradually move to longer visits. Taking small steps like this will give him a chance to learn to self-regulate.

If it is not possible to stay with him, another alternative would be to call him during the visits, even if he is only there for a couple of hours. Call him and check in with him. A quick phone connection can do wonders. Depending on his age, another option would be to send him with a "sensory comfort." This could be a stuffed animal, a locket, a pillow, etc. - something tangible that creates security for him.

Prior to leaving, talk to your son about the visit. Discuss with him the differences between being at home and being away. Explore the feelings that might come up when he is away. Discuss how long he will be away and at what time you will be picking him up. Remember, children need predictability. Reassure him he will be coming back home and that you love him even when he is away from you.

Children's behavior is a communication. His dysregulation that results from being away is telling you that it is simply too much for him. Work to make some of the above modifications, keep the focus on creating security, predictability, and connection.

Q: *While trying to embrace my daughter (age 13) during stressful times, I began to realize that she has created crises over and over to receive love and attention. It usually happens when I have a plan and it did not include her (work, coffee with a friend, etc.). She would have a crisis (feel sick, kick the wall and insist on a trip to the E.R., lock herself in her room). Then, when I try to include her in everything, she sabotages it (pushes the table over in the restaurant, breaks equipment at work, ruins clothes in stores at the mall, etc.). I feel like I am being completely controlled and "trained" to focus only on her all of the time. How do I manage this?*

A: There are several dynamics going on in the relationship between you and your daughter. First, let us look beyond the behavior to determine why children "create crises." The voice of this type of behavior is saying, "I need to feel loved and I need to have attention so I know I won't be lost in this world!"

Behavior is the language of our children. As adults, we communicate verbally and miss the voice of our children because these behaviors interrupt the flow of our day and are often so nerve grinding, we cannot listen to them.

Your daughter is expressing that she is insecure in her attachment relationship with you. When you leave home without her, the acting out or sicknesses begins. Although I do not have her exact history, this tells me that she has experienced a significant attachment break in the past. She is terrified of you leaving her...it feels like you will not come back.

Her perception and fear of you leaving her is more than just an idea; it is her reality. Our thoughts become our reality. Try to relate to her fear in a situation in your life. If you were convinced, for some reason, that your life partner would be injured in a car accident on his way to work, you would do EVERYTHING in your power to keep him/her from leaving the house. You might yell in desperation to get him/her to understand the seriousness of this issue. You might even feign an illness in your efforts to have him/her stay home with you.

This is your daughter's story. Her fear of losing you is driving these behaviors.

Then, when you take her with you, you take her out of desperation on your part. So, even though she was with you, I suspect you are not 100% present with her. You do not want her there because this is supposed to be your time to take care of yourself and you feel like you do not have any other choice but to take her with you.

This is all understandable, and unfortunately, happens too many times to parents simply out of their own need for survival.

So you take her with you and all the while the monsters of resentment, anger, regressive attitude of "whatever," and intolerance raise their ugly heads. These stressors become barriers to your connection with her. You are physically with her, but not emotionally engaged and not paying attention to her from an intrinsic, core level within you.

Your daughter is very intuitive; she can sense the barriers of your resentment and your state of survival. If you are in a place of survival, you cannot be in a place of unconditional love for someone else. Your focus is on you, leaving no emotional space for your child and rendering you unable to respond to

■

If you are in a place of survival, you cannot be in a place of unconditional love for someone else.

■

your child in an authentic and personal way.

Due to her intense fear of losing you, she needs you to connect with her at every level possible. This means connecting with her through your metacommunication (your tone of voice, timing of your responses, inflection in your voice, your physical touch, your body posture and body language, your facial expressions, your eye contact, etc.). **It takes using all of your senses to fully be in relationship with your child to create security with a child who is so overtly insecure.**

When you are unable to do this, the result is that your daughter is left feeling even more unsafe, unprotected, and insecure. At this point, you are now in a public place and she is sensing your disconnect and, additionally, she becomes overwhelmed and threatened by being in a new environment. She shifts into a place of complete overwhelm and her behaviors are out of control. The mother /daughter connection is lost, so efforts to regulate her and calm her prove futile.

You become stressed and the public humiliation is making the hair on the back of your neck rise. Your thought process goes something like this, "*@%$ it, she's ruining my time, again! I should have just left her home!" Disaster strikes once again.

There *is* a better way. We know that children become secure when they feel accepted, approved, validated, and acknowledged. It will take sharing some experiences with her, just the two of you, to create this security.

It can be as simple as a "Girl's Night Out" and driving down to have ice cream or something special in a quiet and calm environment, just the two of you. It is not about the ice cream, though. It is about your relationship with her. It requires you to be authentic and fully present with her.

She is old enough to be able to express her fears of you leaving her. Point out what would happen in the past when you left. Let her know that you understand that these behaviors were signals of her being so scared of you leaving. Apologize for not "hearing" her. Commit to making it different with her. Help her to express her fears when you are both calm and regulated. It will help diffuse the ignition of acting out behaviors the next time you leave without her.

Validate her fears. Acknowledge how scary it must feel every time you leave home without her. Accept her reaction to your absence. Reassure her that you want to make this better for her.

The next time you have to leave, spend at least 15 minutes of one-on-one time with her prior to leaving. Set up a plan for her to call you when she feels scared. Make your time away from her short at first. Prolonged absences can be too overwhelming to her regulatory system. You can begin to build on these times away, but start slowly.

Remember that children heal through relationships. Therapeutic worksheets, behavior charts, and logical consequences do not promote in-depth healing. It takes you being 100% present in relationship when you are with her in order for her begin to feel safe when you are not with her.

■

Children heal through relationships.

■

Trauma

Q: *When my son, Robbie, was three and a half, I had a baby who died at birth. I was told that the birth would be uneventful, so we made the decision to have Robbie with us there, which proved to be very traumatic. The baby died and was later taken to the funeral home but Robbie did not understand why we were leaving his baby brother behind. He cried and threw a fit. I understand now why my son started acting out and having a lot of temper tantrums after this experience. He continues to have outbursts of anger over seemingly small things, as well as being unwilling to separate and not wanting me to leave him places, even familiar places. I have been doing my own emotional work, but I know there is more. Any suggestions?*

A: I am sorry to hear how difficult this has been for your entire family. It certainly explains Robbie's inability to regulate and feel safe. So the question is, "What now?" The first place to start is with you, which you are already doing. It will take truly forgiving yourself for anything you perceive as your fault and getting down to the depths of your grief. As you are able to see your own pain, you will be able to absorb Robbie's pain.

This will take talking to Robbie about what happened, perhaps through stories or role-playing. Many times parents are hesitant to talk about these experiences, thinking they will scare their children. But the reality is that our memory systems are designed to store every experience we have. You will not be giving him any new information but allowing him to begin processing the incredible fear that is still in him.

Traumatic experiences are often stored by the right brain in the form of pictures. This is why drawing pictures and using artistic techniques are so powerful, especially with children who had limited vocabularies during early traumatic childhood experiences. Bringing these pictures up to the conscious level, sharing them with you, and having words to describe the feelings of fear, abandonment, and rejection will foster his healing process.

While picture drawing, story telling, and role-playing are helpful, they are only peripheral parts of the process. We heal through relationships, so the key in your situation is to be 100% open to Robbie's pain. Thus, your process is critical to his healing process and the level of the parent/child relationship.

Robbie needs you to talk to him at an emotional level and absorb all the pain he has stored inside. This includes apologizing to him. The apology is simply about taking responsibility for the incident because children need their parents to take responsibility. It is not that you actually did anything intentional, just that here and now you are taking responsibility for the event because he felt completely powerless and, if we are honest with ourselves, he was completely terrified.

Until you are ready to do this and have moved further in your own healing process, I would begin addressing Robbie's fears by talking to his subconscious. If you have to leave him, you can say to him, "I'm going to be gone for a few hours and that really scares you. In fact, it is going to feel like I've left you forever. I understand why it is so scary for you now." If you feel strong enough and ready to handle his emotions, you can even add in, "It is going to feel like I left you, just like when we had to leave your baby brother at the funeral home. That's how scary it is for you when I leave because he never came back." As you connect with his fear, he will not be in it alone, thus will not feel as abandoned or as scared. Sometimes this can be an automatic switch in behavior, sometimes it takes more repetition.

The bottom line is that you cannot deal with the tantrums, simply as tantrums. It will take dealing with the core issue of fear and abandonment driving the tantrums in order to help Robbie firm up his foundation again.

I encourage you to remember that every event in life is a lesson in acceptance and offers us a chance to expand our ability to love and forgive. The irony of this experience is that you had Robbie with you because you were trying to build a strong relationship between him and his brother and build a strong family unit. I want you to see that this opportunity of relationship building has not been lost. It has simply manifested itself in a different and more intense way.

Once you get to the core of Robbie's pain, he will ultimately be more emotionally attuned than most adults in this world.

Q: *My son, age 7, experienced trauma at 18 months. He was under a car leaving his day care provider's house and was briefly dragged before he was discovered. He had no broken bones – but had severe road rash on his legs, requiring surgery and "burn care" over the next 6 weeks. Over the years he has talked about someone "killing him" and that he is afraid to die. Tonight I snuggled with him in bed and he told me he liked that because no scary people could come get him. I told him he was not going to die. He told me he wanted to go to heaven right now because he knew he would be safe there because no one could kill him there. I told him that he was safe here with me. How do I help my son integrate his fear of dying? I can not tell him he will not die and I cannot assure him that I will always be there to protect him. How can I help him feel safe enough that he no longer has these worries?*

A: What an intense experience for your son! He seems very open to talking about this, which is a wonderful start to his healing process. The first concept to recognize is that it is not your job to change his fears...he simply needs space to be able to process it with you. Your responsibility comes in providing the space for him to do this. As you work towards this and relieve yourself of this responsibility, your stress level will decrease, which will then in turn provide him more emotional safety.

> ■
>
> *The first concept to recognize is that it is not your job to change his fears . . . he simply needs space to be able to process it with you.*
>
> ■

One of the best ways to provide emotional safety is by validating his fears. When he expresses his fear of dying, instead of telling him he is not going to die, validate that it must be so scary to feel like that. As parents, we become so uncomfortable with our children's fear, that our response is nothing more than our way of helping ourselves feel better. The focus is then on us and we do or say whatever will help us feel safer. Parenting involves getting outside of our own emotions to meet our child in his space.

Here is a sample dialogue to illustrate this:

Son: "Mom, I sometimes feel like I'm going to die."
Mom: "That must feel so scary." *(with empathy and with a passion for understanding how scary it must feel)*
Son: *(nods his head)*
Mom: "Can I just lay here and cuddle with you while you have all those big fears?"
Son: *(moves closer to mom)*
Mom: "I love you. Share those big scary feelings with me, honey. They're too big to have on your own."

Notice that mom simply validated and offered herself as the regulatory figure to help sooth her son with her emotional awareness and physical touch. She did not work to convince him of anything or to "fix" the situation.

In your question, you asked how you can help him feel safe enough so that he no longer has these worries. To answer this, ask yourself this essential question, "Who is the one most uncomfortable with these worries? Me or him?" Perhaps it is you. Continue to process through your pain in order to create more emotional space for your child's pain.

The most honest place to start is to take responsibility for what happened to your son. This is not to blame you; it is to meet your child in his basic need. "Son, I'm so sorry that I wasn't there to protect you."

You mentioned that you are "telling him now that he is safe here with you, but then what?" He may not be able to trust that you are here now until you take responsibility for not being there then. As you take responsibility, you are removing the responsibility from him (releasing rejecting thoughts such as, *"I must have done something wrong that this happened" or "I need to protect myself better in the future."*). Children need their parents to take responsibility for their experiences in order to move forward in their development safely and comfortably.

Your son is expressing his need to feel safe (reflected in his comment about wanting to be safe in heaven). The more you work to calm your stress and accept that it is his journey to process through his fears with your support, understanding, and validation instead of your solution set, the more he will feel safe. **Paradoxically, the more you try to "fix" it for him, the further from safety you will find yourselves.**

Despite such a tragic event, you will see that as your son processes through it with you, the more insightful he will be of himself and the more of a quest for life he will develop. When life is threatened to such a degree, it is then that we find the desire to live life to its fullest. Keep working to support him and you will see amazing things happen in his development!

Traumatic Birth

Q: *My son, now six years old, is very controlling in his behaviors. His birth experience was difficult. When my wife was eight months pregnant, I received a call from her doctor that she had an aneurism and that he was concerned that she might die and/or that the baby might die. The next month was an incredibly stressful time for our family and my son was born a few weeks later by C-section. I was told that mom and baby were just fine. Could my son be dysregulated even though he has been with us since birth and could this birth experience have anything to do with his behaviors now?*

A: Birth trauma has an incredible impact on our development. I do not believe that we truly understand the depth of such experiences and the influence they have on our physical, emotional, spiritual, and cognitive development for our entire lives. Your son came into this world in terror. He entered life overwhelmed by the fear of death. His mother was fearful not only for her own life but for his life. All those feelings were transferred to his little system. It is important to realize that he did not have the internal resources to handle such an experience and thus, those feelings were stored in the cells of his body (his unconscious memory) and now his system is programmed for survival. His controlling behaviors are a direct reflection of this.

In order to help children process through these early life experiences, they need to hear their story. They need to be able to make sense of what happened and they need to be able to start the process of connecting the emotions with words and cognitive thought. Begin this process by sitting by your wife and having your son laying on your laps, holding him close. Talk to him about what happened when he was in "mommy's tummy." And more importantly, express yourselves to him from a deep emotional level. Words alone will not connect with this time in his life. Trauma happens at the emotional level, especially preverbal trauma such as this example. Allow yourselves to cry and feel the depth of this fear (yours and his).

Let him know that you now realize how scared he was. Let him know that you understand that he was absolutely terrified. Do not be afraid to use the words, "Son, you thought you were going to die." These are not new ideas you are planting in his head. These feelings are already inside of him and he is acting out of them of a daily basis. You will be giving him the words to finally make the connection and thus, helping him to lay the path for healing.

Take ownership of this experience for him by apologizing to him. Children are egocentric and automatically react internally by thinking it is their fault. I would guess that your wife feels a level of guilt and this will help her process through her feelings, opening up the gateway for a deeper level of attachment, thus helping your son ultimately strengthen his bond with you both. As this connection is strengthened, his need to control will dissipate as he will develop a sense of safety and security.

Rebuilding Trust & Relationships

Q: *Do you have any advise on how to rebuild trust? What about a teen that's lying and not being honest about what she is doing and whom she is with? I want to trust her and believe her . . . where do I start?*

A: Mistrust between two people is a breakdown in the safety of the relationship. In this example, the attachment between you and your teenage daughter is strained and in need of repair. In order for parents to reconnect with their teens, parents need to shift to a place of listening, rather than lecturing. Listening and understanding builds relationships and trust. Telling and lecturing creates division. Yet, shifting to a place of listening can be scary—literally terrifying—for parents, because they no longer have the same amount of control over their teens as they did just a few years ago.

■

Listening and understanding builds relationships and trust. Telling and lecturing creates division.

■

I would suggest that you first recognize your own pain and hurt that comes when your teenager lies to you. It can be extremely hurtful and I would encourage you to own this pain and fully acknowledge it. This is a critical part of the process because any feelings you are harboring against your daughter will prevent you from doing the next step successfully. And that next step is to take full responsibility for your part in allowing this relationship to become so strained and distant. Relationships are dyadic in nature; each person has a role in keeping this relationship safe, loving, and connected. Parents have a greater responsibility in this because they are the ones teaching their children how to create these relationships.

So, you want more of the "nuts and bolts" of how to rebuild trust and strengthen a strained relationship? Here is a true story of a mother and her teenage daughter:

One night, mom went to her teenager's room and said, "I haven't spent enough time listening to you and understanding you. I'm sorry our relationship has become so distant. I'd like to change that, so every night at this time, I'd like to spend 20 minutes with you. It will be just our special time together."

The teen then looks at mom as if mom has three eyeballs and says "I don't want you in here." So mom, now in a place of listening instead of lecturing and correcting, interprets this kind of negative and disrespectful talk simply as a sign of how broken this relationship really is at this point.

Not taking her daughter's response personally, the parent replies, "Okay, honey, but I'll be right outside your door waiting for you when you're ready." Mom then sits down in the hallway, next to a closed door (Mom realizes this closed door is a telling symbol of the closed relationship between the two of them). For 20 minutes she sits and every so often mom taps on the door to let the teen know she is still there. Each night at the same time, mom repeats this process with the teen, sitting outside the teen's room.

Finally, seven days later, the teen swings the door open and says with her big attitude, "Well, come on in!" That is mom's invitation to connect with her teen!

Less than three weeks after this invitation, both mom and her teenage daughter are talking and building an incredibly close relationship. As this relationship builds, the teen then develops a sense of wanting to please her parent rather than rebelling against rules and limits. Boundaries are absolutely necessary and important for our children. The goal in connecting with our children is to help them develop internal controls to stay within these boundaries. When a child becomes unresourced and dysregulated internally, the parent is there to help the child regulate and feel resourced again. It is far more effective to learn to regulate through relationships, than through consequences.

We have to meet our teens where they are in order to create safety in our relationships with them. We need to move out of trying to control them and into being connected in order to influence them. Relationships are not about control; they are about loving influence.

> ■
>
> *As this relationship builds, the teen then develops a sense of wanting to please her parent rather than rebelling against rules and limits.*
>
> ■

Q: *My child is lonely but sabotages relationships. How do you help a child who sabotages play times and creates her own loneliness?*

A: It is a natural reaction for children and adults to be in conflict over the need to be in relationships, yet simultaneously, to be terrified of them. We are designed to be in relationship with one another because being in relationship ensures our survival. It is a fact that we are stronger as a group of people than as individuals. Yet, it is in a close relationship that we can also experience the most pain and rejection. What a dichotomy!

Your daughter is seeking friendships, yet once she enters into these friendships, she becomes overwhelmed and scared of being rejected. In order to create safety for herself and to not be rejected, she becomes the one to reject her friends. Perfect plan. She is no longer vulnerable. However, the long-term effect is that she is without friends and is lonely.

It is important to remember that social situations are some of the most stressful situations we experience, both as children and adults. Not only is there the threat of being rejected and made fun of, but being with other children can be overstimulating to the nervous system, leaving children feeling overwhelmed and out of control. The more dysregulated the other children are, the worse it is.

The environment also plays a significant role in how well your child can handle social situations. Consider being at an outdoor playground with only three children with lots of room to run and play. Now consider being at a Chuck E. Cheese on Saturday morning with eight different birthday parties going on simultaneously with all the blinking lights, loud noises, and excited children. In which environment would it be easier to maintain your regulation? Never underestimate the power of the environment.

In order to teach her how to relate with friends and stay safe, you will need to help her during social interactions. Plan a play date with one child (preferably a child who has some self-regulatory ability). Play with them together at first, helping your daughter to feel safe. If she appears to be handling the interaction well, have the two children play together without you but stay within close proximity. Let your daughter know she can come get you at anytime if she needs you. Limit the first play date to about 30 minutes. Repeat this process a few times, each time increasing the amount of time they play together.

At first, keeping your daughter in your home environment is ideal as this is her safe base. When she has experienced several safe interactions with a friend, you might venture to set up a play date at the other child's home. However, do not leave her there alone at the beginning. She needs you there, even if you are in another room visiting with the other parent. Your daughter needs to know that you are in close proximity and that she has the ability to come to you when she gets overwhelmed. Pulling her into you for a "time-in" can help bring her back to a place of balance before going back to playing.

Each interaction will provide her with a positive social experience. These are replacement experiences that will build safety and security over previous experiences of feeling scared and overwhelmed. Take baby steps in providing her the opportunity to learn how to stay regulated and feel safe in these interactions. Eventually, she will be able to develop the regulatory ability to handle more friends for a longer period of time. You will be helping her develop the vital skill of social interaction – a skill that will serve her well into adulthood.

Rage, Aggression, Destruction & Hate

Q: *Recently, our nine-year-old son has begun threatening his father and me when he does not get his way or gets upset. I find myself pulling back from him and feeling scared to be alone with him. I realize that my history of growing up with an alcoholic father and disruptive older brother tie into my present feelings. My son was also hurt as a child and I wasn't able to protect him. Now I find myself at a loss as to what to do.*

A: When children are feeling threatened, they may behave in a threatening way. Your son's behaviors directly correlate to his emotional state of fear and a feeling of being powerless. From what you are describing, he is a hyper-sensitive child with a reactive response system.

Parenting him will require you and your husband taking responsibility for this hyper-sensitivity – someone has to. He cannot at this point. Whether or not what happened in the past was your "fault", is insignificant. At nine years old, your son needs a fresh start. Give him the freedom for this to happen by taking responsibility and saying to him, "I take full responsibility for you. **I take full responsibility for what happened to you and all that you give me.**"

We live in a blame-based society, so this can be a difficult concept. The reality is that fear does not exist on a linear timeline. His fear of you now is enmeshed with previous fear-driven experiences in his past. He cannot make a separation in order to classify and organize past fear from present fear. He is living in a disorganized state of fear – it is all present fear to him. Thus, he needs you to take ownership and responsibility of all of this fear and pain for him.

In applying this to your interactions with your son, it means you have to enter into relationship with him expecting nothing in return, only absorbing his fear and pain. When he threatens you, this is your opportunity to absorb it for him. You will actually want to invite him to give you more of the pain (working to help him channel this fear into words), saying words like, "Something I've done has threatened you. I'm listening, honey. I need to know more about your fear."

■

Your fear is creating more fear in your son.

■

What makes this so difficult is that your belief system says that your son is going to hurt you; but this is not reality. Unfortunately, our minds create beliefs that then create our reality. Here's the good news: **Not everything your mind tells you is true.** In fact, most of what your mind tells you is not true and you have to work to cancel these beliefs and override them with truths.

When you look at your son, say to yourself, "He is not going to kill me." Your fear is a false interpretation of past experiences (linked to either your brother or father). You have to stay in the present moment by saying, "This is my son, not my brother and definitely not my father." Realize that your fear is creating more fear in your son so it is imperative to make this separation in your mind and heart.

Can you imagine your mother being scared of you? This feeds a child's primal fear of being rejected and abandoned. Your fear is scaring him even more. The only response he knows to give in return is to threaten you and your husband. When you or your husband to him with power and control, a negative neurological feedback loop is in full swing.

To break this loop, it will take you shifting into a place of understanding and unconditional acceptance. When you can remain in this place with your son, you will not be worried about what to say or what to do. Simply being present with him is all that needs to happen at this point. If you are emotionally safe, he will know it and he will lead you through the conversation. Listen to him-really listen to him. If you get to a point of complete loss and want to say something, reassure him and take responsibility for his fear and pain. **"I love you. I'm so sorry for what happened to you. I'm sorry I couldn't keep you from getting hurt."**

Q: *Why is my child so destructive?*

A: Studies have shown that children who were abused demonstrate a significantly higher incidence of self-destructive behaviors than children who were never abused. Additionally, children who were abused are also much more destructive than children who were neglected. The physical expression of emotions becomes a child's framework for releasing stress; thus, physically destroying things and property are often part of the child's *modus operandi*.

I would suspect that your child is more destructive when he is stressed out, as well. We all become more destructive when we are stressed. There is a part in each one of us that has a self-destructive theme. In most people, this perfectly natural self-destruct part is dormant and sleeps unless extreme conditions awaken it under stress.

When we as adults get stressed out and lose the balance in our lives, we neglect changing the oil in our car, we stop working out, we feed our bodies with junk food, and we pay our bills late. We do not care at the moment; we are simply trying to get through our day and have no concern for the future.

Your child's destructive actions follow the same path. He doesn't have the insight at the moment to consider that breaking his toy will result in him not having something to play with in the future. There is no future for him. It is all about him being upset in the moment and he will do whatever it takes to release his feelings. Giving him logic about why he should not be destructive will only fuel his need to be destructive.

Destructive behaviors are prevalent in the animal kingdom. A scorpion surrounded by flames will sting itself in the back and kill itself rather than be burned to death. Likewise, when children no longer value life or themselves, they will turn against themselves or become destructive in the world in which they live.

When children destroy their own possessions, consider that such tangible items are representations of who they are. The receipt of a shiny new toy for a child who feels unworthy and unlovable is in total conflict with his neurological program that says, "I'm worthless, I'm a piece of garbage, and I don't even deserve the crumbs on my plate." The child tears up and breaks the toy in order to make his external world match his internal reality.

If we consequent this behavior, we are only adding more fear to a child who has bottomed out in his level of self-control and self-esteem. Punishing a child in this state is completely illogical. Implementing the *Beyond Consequences* model, focusing on connecting in relationship and helping reduce the child's stress in his environment, will help reduce these destructive tendencies. Developing a relationship based in unconditional love, acceptance, validation, acknowledgment, and security will help shift your child out of this internal state of worthlessness to a state of self-love, self-acceptance, and self-worth.

Help him shift his physical expression of fear into a verbal dialogue with you. Give him permission to be angry and finally have a voice-to be heard. Be proactive and stay attuned to when he is reaching his window of stress tolerance. Work to interrupt this cycling of stress within his system.

Remember that when he destroys his things, it is not about you. I realize it is difficult to watch your child tear up his new birthday toy that you picked out especially for him – that you managed to buy above and beyond your normal budget. He does love you and appreciate you; he simply needs to learn how to love himself before he can show you appreciation for what you have given him.

Q: *Why do dysregulated children often target eye glasses and eye wear to break or steal when stressed?*

A: When someone looks us in the eyes, it heightens our sensory system. This can be a positive experience if you are having a romantic meal and staring eye to eye with your lover. It heightens the connection.

Conversely, this visual connection can be a negative experience if you are already in a heightened state of stress. As discussed in Chapter 11 of *Beyond Consequences, Logic, and Control, Volume 1,* the eyes are sensory pathways. We know from brain research that the most direct way to stimulate the frontal lobe of the brain is through eye contact. This part of our brain is directly involved with the body's stress response system.

When children are stressed out, eye contact can exasperate the child's stress level. Since most children with trauma histories live at an intense level, they will go to extremes in order to reduce sensory stimulation because they literally hurt when experiencing this amount of pain...they have reached their window of stress tolerance.

Aiming for the eye glasses is a way to say, "Stop looking at me! It's too much! If you look at me any longer, I'm going to blow! Stop looking at me NOW!"

I believe that we also need to consider the nonverbal communication being expressed when a parent and child are in the heat of a dysregulated moment. What does the parent look like? Does the parent look approachable? What are the parent's body, facial expressions, and shape of the eyes communicating?

The eyes can be a source of sensory discomfort at many levels.

Are the nonverbal signals communicating, "I am mad at you," or "I'm really disappointed in you," or "I can't believe what you are doing"? If so, the natural reaction of the child is to get the parent not to look at him because these messages are hitting the core of his issues (fear of rejection, fear of abandonment, fear of not being good enough, etc.).

Have you ever had an experience when someone was looking at you while angry or upset with you? How did it make you feel? The negativity communicated through the eyes probably made you feel even more dysregulated. Maybe you can remember a time when someone you did not even know was staring at you. Did it make you feel uncomfortable? Perhaps in your mind you were saying, "I just wish he would stop looking at me!" The eyes can be a source of sensory discomfort at many levels.

If your child has had a history of having difficulty with eye contact during times of heightened stress, be mindful to not look directly at him during these moments. Stay emotionally present with him, but move your eyes away from him directly, just looking down a bit or off to the side of him. If he is looking away from you, join him by diverting your eyes in the same place he is looking.

Q: *My eight-year-old son "hates" everything: the particular car driving down the street, the shirt I'm wearing, the kid next door, the color of the living room, the cashier at the grocery store, etc. I am* *having trouble understanding this and how to deal with it. Any insights?*

A: I imagine this is a maddening place to be with your son and that it feels as if nothing will make him happy. It may feel as if anything positive you try is met with resistance and negativity.

In order to reverse your child's perception of the world as negative, you must first gain a new understanding of why he "hates" everything. When children's needs are met early in their development, their program for the world becomes positive and optimistic. When a baby is crying and sending out stress signals, he is in need of nurturing and comforting care. When this is given to him, his system is shifted back to a state of regulation and the world is a good place. He develops a sense of optimism.

If he is not cared for in the way that fits his needs or if he is left on his own to navigate through his internal stress, the world becomes a scary place. Negative repetitious conditioning breeds an outlook of pessimism. No matter how much he cries, no matter what he does, he feels as if he cannot convince his caretakers to help him. Helplessness and overwhelm prevail. For such a child, nothing is working, so his universal program of "nothing being right" is being created.

> ■
> *Negative repetitious conditioning breeds an outlook of pessimism.*
> ■

A child who "hates" everything is a child in a perpetual state of fear and dysregulation. His neurophysiological system has been programmed to see the world as half empty instead of half full. He truly does not know that everything is going to be all right. He really does not know that good always overcomes evil. Essentially, he is programmed to live an operatic tragedy instead of a light-hearted drama.

Think about this . . . isn't it great to simply go to the video store and check out what kind of movie you want? Maybe it is a romantic comedy; maybe it is an action movie; maybe even during Halloween season it is a horror flick.

But in our own realities, we do not have the luxury of returning one life and checking out another so quickly. What we do have are three key elements to make significant changes to our life stories: 1) understanding, 2) relationship, and 3) plasticity.

The first of these, understanding, was addressed in the beginning of the response to this question. The second, relationships, is something that is always available to initiate. Healing happens in the context of relationships, and most fervently through the context of the parent-child relationship. And third, plasticity, is what an eight-year-old has plenty of. The brain continues to make major changes until we are at least 25 years old.

Your child needs to know that the world is safe and good. In order to make this happen, you will need to create a deeper relationship with him. You will need to help him to express himself at a deeper level. The next time he makes a negative statement, such as, "I hate the shirt you are wearing," sit with him and listen to him. Ask him more about what he hates.

Validate his negativity instead of trying to convince him of something more positive. "You really do hate this shirt. Wow. Let me know how much you hate it. Tell me more." As he expresses himself, help him shift into the feelings behind these words. "How does that make you feel?"

> ■
>
> *Healing happens in the context of relationships, and most fervently through the context of the parent-child relationship.*
>
> ■

Essentially, his "I hate the world" statements are indicators of his own internal reality: "The world hates me and I don't even deserve to be in this world." When a child (or adult) feels this depth of darkness from within himself, it makes sense that all his comments about his external environment are negative.

Think about a time when you were just in a bad mood. Nothing seemed to be right; nothing seemed to be the way you wanted it to be. Your perception of the world matched your negative framework. So, it is the same with your child, simply at a deeper level within the core of his being.

When you can help him to move into this core area within himself by listening, validating, maximizing, tolerating, accepting, and staying present with him, you will be there in relationship to guide him towards feeling safe and loved. Thus, you will be able to guide him to see that the world is good and hope does exist. It will take positive repetitious conditioning to do this for him (see *Beyond Consequences, Logic, and Control, Volume 1, Chapter 3*).

The reason this works is because our neurological systems are "plastic." We have the ability to change and be molded, especially children. Your son is growing and developing everyday. He still has years ahead of him to create new neuropathways. Every interaction with you is an opportunity to literally change his brain and lay down new neuropatterns of positive thought and positive outlook.

Work to stay in a place of understanding, keep yourself regulated, and know that through loving influence, you have the ability to create exactly the environment he needs for healing, hope, and optimism.

Q: *My son (11 years old) has always destroyed his toys. Lately, it's intensified. Almost every day, I find bits and pieces cut-off, missing, or ripped off from toys. When asked why, my son always says, "I don't know." This is really becoming a big issue. I get very upset. I even swore he'll have nothing for Christmas. To which he answered "You've already said that, and it's not true." I feel awful, of course, but what can I do?*

A: Traditionally, the interpretation of such behavior would be that your son is willfully doing this and that this "pushing your buttons" is an enjoyable activity for him. Advice from therapists and parent coaches would sound something like this:

"Stop buying him things and strip the room. He needs to stop his behavior more than he needs to have belongings to destroy. And you need to help him figure the issues out more than you need to be aggravated by his pushing your buttons – which he apparently has figured out how to do and enjoys."

This type of advice does not take into consideration the understanding we now have of how the brain functions. This traditional advice is behaviorally focused and it assumes that this child can access all three brains during this time of toy destruction (see *Beyond Consequences, Logic, and Control, Volume 2, Chapter 2)*. The reality is that he cannot. He is operating from the two parts of the brain that work on autopilot.

Remember that our higher level of thinking, stationed in the neocortex, is only accessible when we are calm and regulated. This clearly is a child who is stressed out and unable to think rationally and reasonably. He truly does not know why he is breaking his toys and to ask him to explain himself is like asking a kindergarten to do calculus. Remember that our level of awareness and our conscious motor control and "will" are found in the neocortex.

Many times it is simply the volume of toys and others items that we give our children that becomes too much for them to handle. In such an overwhelming environment, things are just lost, stomped on or ruined.

Simplicity fosters regulation. In a culture of consumerism and materialism, it takes mindfulness to create simplicity in our homes for us and for our children. It is an art but your children will benefit from a sense of organization and order.

For children whose emotional age is lower than their chronological age, simplicity it necessary. When you were a baby, your life was simple. You wanted only things that you needed; food, water, and to be cleaned up. When you received those things you smiled and reacted with love and felt the warmth of acceptance. It does not take much to make a baby happy. He is not looking to buy the new iPhone or a new X-box game.

So, keep this in mind with your children. As the great architect Mies van der Rohe said, "Less is more."

In your frustration of not being able to make this situation different, you have made threats to your child. When the concern for our own well-being becomes greater than the concern for our child, we have shifted out of a state of love and into a state of fear. That is why this feels, as you described, "awful."

This feeling of awful is your body's gauge to let you know that you have shifted. When your car is running out of fuel, the little red light turns on. This is your little red light that is indicating that what you are doing is not out of love, but out of fear. Moving out of this place of fear takes understanding how to help your child, instead of how to threaten your child.

As mentioned in Chapter 1, it takes asking the right question. Instead of asking, "How do I get my child to stop this behavior?" You have to ask, "What is driving my child's behavior?"

When your child is playing, check in with him periodically in order to interrupt his stress cycle. Set time aside and play with him. Help him stay regulated and engaged in relationship so that he does not get "lost" in the play experience.

Show him how to play with toys and how to work through aggravating times during the play experience when he cannot seem to get the toy to do what he wants it to do. If he gets too engrossed in a toy, reassure him he is okay. Sometimes we want something to go just the way we envision it and it becomes a fixation to make it happen; a toy may be broken in the process.

His internal dialogue is saying, "You're not alright. You're not okay. You must make this work in order to be okay." Rewrite his script by letting him know through your love, patience, and understanding that he is alright and that he has always been alright.

> ■
>
> *Play is a child's work so too much at one time can be overwhelming to his nervous system.*
>
> ■

Monitor his stress level by staying attuned to his emotional state. Interrupt the play time with a walk, a snack, or a conversation. Play is a child's work so too much at one time can be overwhelming to his nervous system. Help him become attuned to his internal level of stress. Teach him how to breath in order to calm himself down. This is a skill that will serve him well throughout his life.

If you are correlating your child's success at his play to your success as a parent, then your work comes in validating yourself first as a parent, regardless of your child's behavior. Your ability to acknowledge yourself as a good parent is your responsibility and not to be based on the outcome of your child's ability to stay regulated when he plays.

Feelings of, "I bought that for you and now you go and tear it up!" are feelings for you to address. Feeling as if your buttons are being pushed is a time for you to understand yourself even better. I would suspect there is a dormant experience from your past that is being awakened and the feelings that accompany it need to be acknowledged and processed.

The next time you, as an adult, are not taking care of your "toys" like not getting your oil changed on time, remember that this comes from a place of being overly stressed and overwhelmed. Stay attuned to this within yourself and there you will find a deeper understanding of your child.

Manipulation

Q: *My child can be amazingly manipulative, all the time! If I lovingly respond to her, am I not just reinforcing this behavior?*

A: Manipulation is a communication for connection with the parent. Paradoxically, when our children demonstrate this behavior, it does quite the opposite to us. It creates an uneasy feeling within us, constricts us, and in many cases, repulses us away from our child.

Let's step back and look at early childhood interactions between the mother and her infant. There is where we will find the roots of manipulative behavior, thus giving us the ability to create a new understanding.

The first relationship an infant is designed to experience is the relationship with his mother. This relationship begins in the womb and is designed to continue at a high level of intensity for at least the next three years of her life. It is in these first three years that amazing development and connection happens due to his mother's attention, attunement, and devotion to him.

As discussed in Chapter 2, these mother/child interactions occur primarily in the right brain. The right brain holds the capacity for emotional and non-verbal information processing while the left-brain holds the capacity for language and logical processing. For the infant and young child, with no or limited language skills, communication happens primarily in the right brain. These experiences occur at the emotional level, not at the cognitive or "thinking" level.

Thus, the communication between the mother and child happens at a non-verbal level. **When the child gives signals to his mother, he experiences his mother as predictable and manipulatable.** Infants and young children have this amazing ability to "manipulate" their caretakers. For example, the baby smiles at his mother, the mother smiles back. The baby has created this mirroring response from the mother. The mother will even talk a crazy language like, "Goo-goo-gaa-gaa" to the baby. No one else on this planet can get this mother to do such things.

The baby can also cry and become hyper-aroused, "manipulating" the caregiver to come over and pick him up. Babies even have this manipulation technique down so well that they can get their parents up from a dead sleep in the middle of the night to feed them. Money and bribes would not even get many of us out of bed in the middle of the night.

Even more impressive, babies can get grown men, CEO's of mega-corporations, dressed in red power ties, to bend over and make silly noises and change their tone of voice to that of a little child. The high-powered, influential board of directors of such a CEO does not even have this kind of power.

You have experienced this yourself. How many times have you walked by a baby, felt this force pulling you over to her, and then dropped everything you were doing to connect with the baby?

This ability to "manipulate" is an important part of any child's development. It is in this attachment system between the mother and the child that the mother is helping the child regulate his states of stress and fear. The mother who attends to her child's negative states is helping her child shift back into a positive state. This is known as "affect synchrony." Affect synchrony is the regulatory means for developing and maintaining positive emotional states within the relationship of emotional communication. Positive states are amplified and maximized for the child while negative states are minimized and neutralized for the child.

> ■
>
> *It is in this attachment system between the mother and the child that the mother is helping the child regulate his states of stress and fear.*
>
> ■

Many times, children miss early life experiences of affect synchrony with their caretaker. This happens all too often when mothers are depressed or overwhelmed as it leaves them emotionally unavailable to their child. Realize that this is a vital part of a child's development and the child will seek to have these experiences even at an older age. Manipulation is simply an inherent way for the child to achieve this goal.

It is important to shift from seeing this as a negative and irritating behavior to that of a request for connection and healing. In doing so, the parent will be able to meet the child in a positive and loving way.

For your daughter, focus on seeing her through the lens of a child who is desperate to know connection and who needs to know what unconditional love is. She needs to know that she is important enough to be able to move you, just like when the baby smiles and the mother smiles back. This gives her a sense of worth and "all-rightness."

Remember to spend time with her, simply playing with her. Playing with her and being with her can repair the missing pieces from developmental history, at a physiological and emotional level. You will also be creating the essential ingredient of life: Joy! By amplifying the positive experiences in her life and by giving her a sense of safety and security in her relationship with you, the need to be manipulative will disappear.

Q: *Because our son is a "master manipulator and liar," how do we know he is telling us the truth during a healing moment?*

A: Let us first look at why a child manipulates. From the child's perspective, manipulation works to:

1. Get what he wants from his parent, believing the parent is not willing to give it to him.
2. Involve the parent in his fear so that he does not have to face it alone.
3. Control and overpower the parents in order to do what he wants them to do because of a feeling of helplessness.
4. Passively take charge because he is scared of the parent. The child believes he needs to retain control of his life so he does not get hurt again.

Manipulative children are scared children. The more intense the manipulation, the more intense the fear state behind the manipulation. Lying has the same roots. The child's subconscious thought process is: "If I lie to my mom, she won't be mad at me. I'll be the hero, and I'll be loved."

These are "survival" techniques your child has developed in order to have his needs met and to be given a sense of "I'm alright." There is a level of insecurity in his relationship with you. He has not yet understood and experienced the safety of unconditional love fully and completely.

The goal, therefore, is not to stop the manipulation, but to create security and safety. Once your child feels secure and knows that your love is real, genuine, and everlasting, the need for manipulative behaviors will disintegrate. Creating the security in your relationship with him will involve listening, validating, and maximizing.

When he is telling you something and your immediate fear is, "I don't know whether or not to believe him." I want you to move past this and simply meet him where he is in that moment. Listen to his story without trying to discern whether or not it is true. Just listen. Validate how he must have felt during the event being described. You are not validating the story, but validating the feelings behind the story. Words like, "Wow! That must have been really scary!" Or "My goodness! You certainly must have felt fantastic saving Suzy from that monster!"

Maximize on the emotional experience behind the story. When a child makes up a story, the story is typically based on real and authentic feelings he is or was having even if the event is fictitious. Your child is working to involve you in his emotional state because it is too big to have on his own. He simply does not realize that he can have your involvement without the lies and manipulation. What hard work he is doing to connect with you!

Remember that manipulation can no longer be manipulation if you are aware of it being manipulation. Listen, validate, and maximize the emotional experience with your son.

Once you are able to give him this prescription of security, the emotional turmoil within him will begin to settle down. He will be able to think more clearly so you can then suggest to him that you are always available to help absorb his pain and that your number one job is to provide him with safety and love. You might say, "It is my job to keep you safe. Please tell me what is going on in your life. Otherwise, if I don't have this information, I can't do my best for you."

Give him the permission to ask you for help and to ask you for a hug when he is feeling scared. In doing this, you are suggesting to him that the need to lie and manipulate is no longer a requirement and he can be completely straightforward with you.

The process of creating a safe parent/child relationship always begins with our own self-understanding.

If you find yourself reacting to this advice or find it difficult to implement the next time you perceive that he is manipulating you, examine this within yourself. The process of creating a safe parent/child relationship always begins with our own self-understanding. Perhaps you had a previous relationship where someone manipulated you. Or perhaps you yourself used to manipulate in order to get your needs met as a child and this mirror into the past is difficult to face.

Your son may be the "master manipulator," but you have the capacity to be the master parent, creating safety and security that will penetrate far beyond the controlling and manipulative behaviors.

Q: *I belong to several adoption list groups on the Internet. The most common issue I read about is manipulation. It came up again this morning when an adoptive parent wrote that her daughter, who has been home for five weeks, peed in her pants while the mother was talking on the phone. The mother made her wash her own pants and take a bath by herself. The mother expressed that her daughter was "manipulative." What is your opinion of the word manipulation?*

A: This interpretation of manipulation from this child who has only been home for five weeks goes beyond my window of stress tolerance! This child is in no way secure enough to be thinking rationally in a way to test her mother. She is living in a deep fear state. This child was too scared and dysregulated to be able to do anything different than what she did.

This child has been through so much transitional trauma that she has disconnected from her body. When pain becomes too great, we literally leave ourselves. Her bodily response of peeing was not connected at the level of thinking.

This behavior is simply a sign that the child needs help connecting with her body. Adding more fear into an already stressed-out, disconnected child, will not create regulation or attachment. All the energy this mother spent in giving the directives to her daughter to clean up and bath herself could have been well served to simply acknowledge her child's fear and calm her child.

Mom needs to recognize how scary it must have felt for her daughter to be ignored while she was on the phone. Mom should help her daughter know that while she is on the phone, Mom has not forgotten her. Adopted children have a high sensitivity to rejection and abandonment. The next time mom is on the phone, she can simply hold her daughter in her lap and stay physically connected with her in order to provide safety. Creating new experiences of love and understanding for her daughter will give her daughter the opportunity to develop self-regulatory skills.

Parenting requires us to go beyond the manipulating – beyond the behavior. Instead of addressing the manipulating behavior, connect with your child to help him work through the stress in his life. Recognize behavior simply as a communication of something deeper.

Bribery

Q: *Is bribery an acceptable tactic to motivate "regulation"?*

A: Let us first look at the definition of bribery. The definition of bribery is a crime implying a sum or gift given that alters the behavior of a person in ways not consistent with the duties of that person. That is an interesting definition of a tactic that we sometimes use with our children.

Consider the fact that we would be using something, which is actually defined as a crime, in order to alter our children's behavior. Think about that. No, I do not believe it is acceptable to use bribery mainly because it is simply addressing the child at the behavioral level.

So, we go back to understanding how stress impacts our children. We know that behavior arises from an emotional place due to stress and fear. If we are only addressing the behavior, we are never connecting and calming the stress that is actually driving this behavior. We have to trust that children inherently want to make appropriate choices. They want to have good behavior. Our children want to please us. It may not always seem that way; in fact it may seem outright malicious that they are not doing what they are supposed to be doing, but at a greater level they are designed to be in relationship. They are designed to be regulated humans. In order to help us get back to this very core level, it is going to take more positive, love-based approaches. Bribery or sticker charts are superficial and are an ineffective means of addressing a child's well-being.

It is similar to the analogy of an iceberg. If you are floating along in the ocean, what you see is the top of the iceberg. What you do not see is the entire iceberg that is underneath the water. The analogy is that our children's behavior is similar to the top of the iceberg that you see. What we do not see is everything that is underneath the iceberg. If we want to get rid of this iceberg, as we want to get rid of our children's negative behaviors, would we chip away at the top of the iceberg? No, we would not even come close to getting rid of the iceberg – just like we cannot chip away and bribe our children into different behavior. It is not going to make a significant difference long term.

What is going to make a difference with an iceberg is chopping away at the bottom of the iceberg. We start addressing the stress at the bottom- the stress that is creating the negative behavior. When we are to able chip away at the bottom of the iceberg, the iceberg gets out of balance and it falls over and it disappears. The same happens with our children when we start addressing their stress and fear. The behaviors are going to disappear. The negative behaviors will not exist because there is no need for them to exist once we have met our children's needs and calmed them through our relationship with them.

The primary purpose of parenting is to be connected to our children. We cannot accomplish this through bribery. The only way we can connect is through love, understanding, commitment, patience, kindness, and being a responsible parent to our children rather than a reactive parent. Bribery is a reactive technique to get children to behave and fails to address our children at the deeper emotional level in which they function.

We also have to understand that regulation is a natural, organic process. To impose something on the outside, such as bribery, is ineffective in order to create something that naturally exists within the internal body. Regulation happens through safe relationships. Regulation happens when we are calm and we know that we are okay. Regulation happens when we know that no matter what we do or how we act that we are always going to be acceptable in our parent's eyes. Bribery gives exactly the opposite message. For a child with a high sensitivity to stress, bribery will most likely ignite dysregulation as opposed to motivate regulation.

■

For a child with a high sensitivity to stress, bribery will most likely ignite dysregulation as opposed to motivate regulation.

■

Hyperactivity

Q: *My soon to be three-year-old was 20 months when she came home from an orphanage. She has always been my little "adrenalin junkie" – she likes to have fun. As she gets older, she is becoming increasingly loud, wild, and bossy. Is this just normal two to three year old behavior? Is hypomania a feature of post-institutional behavior?*

A: Your daughter's behaviors are indicative of a child who is having a difficult time regulating her internal system. It sounds as if her system is in full operation all the time and lacks the internal mechanisms to slow down.

Early childhood deprivation of an attuned parent figure on a consistent basis can cause a child's system to stay in "overdrive." It will take interrupting this cycle for your daughter, otherwise you are likely to continue to see an increase in her level of activity because the body simply does not know a different way of functioning.

Unfortunately, many children are left untreated and, by the time they enter Kindergarten, they are labeled the "bad" child or the "ADHD" child, put on medications and struggle for the rest of their formative years in school.

Fortunately, you have the ability as the parent to make this different for your daughter. This is a great time because her system is so "malleable" at this early age. It begins with understanding that children are not born with the ability to self-regulate. They need a parent or caregiver to help them learn to settle their systems down. Hence, a baby who is crying is fed, held, rocked, and cradled by the parent. The parent is responsible for modulating the child's stress states.

As the child experiences these calming interactions with the parent, the child's neurological system becomes programmed with positive experiences. For a child who does not have an active parent helping her calm the stress, the system never learns to shut off and is in a perpetual state of overwhelm.

To interrupt this stress state, your daughter needs to experience what she did not experience when she was younger. Have her be near you more so you are physically helping to regulate her through your presence. Rock her and bottle feed her. She needs this from you. Such bonding experiences you create are priceless.

Gently pull her into you when she gets overly active and have some "time-In" with her. Reduce the stimulation in the environment (turn off the TV, reduce the lighting, etc.). Decrease the amount of physical space by closing the door of the room you are in or have her come sit with you in a smaller room of the house. Create an external environment that is calm and relaxing and her internal system will learn to settle down.

Help her to learn to express herself, even at 20 months, through facial expressions, tone of voice, and other non-verbal clues. Work to develop your relationship with her, which will ensure the optimal development of your daughter's emotional and physiological regulation.

Any child who is acting this hyper, whether a "normal" two year-old or one who has experienced early years in an orphanage, is a child who needs more parental interaction in order to help the child develop a stronger regulatory system. It is not about behavior; it is about equipping the child to learn to self-regulate and enlarge the child's window of stress tolerance.

Q: *How can we tell if our child is hyper due to dysregulation or if she is just being a kid?*

A: My first response to this question is to ask another question: Does it make a difference? When a child is dysregulated, no matter the cause, responding in a way that will support him, understand him, and teach him how to shift back to a place of regulation should be the parent's primary goal.

I believe that we, as a society, have bought into the "he's just being a kid" mentality too easily. Writing off behavior or stereotyping a type of behavior ignores the individual needs of the child. Nicknames for developmental stages, such as "the terrible two's," keep us in a place to expect such behaviors and to normalize these behaviors. This places us at a distance from our child, rather than motivating us to stay connected with our child during these difficult moments. *Oh, what healing moments are often lost because of these cultural justifications!*

The fact that such behaviors are given a name or a jingle is precisely because they are some of the most difficult times for our children. Staying at bay instead of moving into relationship during these times is the least productive approach and the most damaging. If your child is dysregulated, then he is outside his window of stress tolerance. The most effective way for him to move back into a state of balance and love is to have a parent figure who is regulated to help him shift back through this relational connection.

Asking a child to shift back on his own, especially children with limited regulatory abilities and limited experiences of understanding what regulation feels like, is a high expectation. For some children, this is an impossible expectation. This unrealistic expectation is what often leads to the magnitude and intensity of frustration parents have with their children.

So, to directly answer this question, it is pointless to distinguish between a child who is hyper and a child who is "just being a kid." They are one and the same. A child acting inappropriately is a dysregulated child who is outside of his relationship with his parent(s). When the relationship is intact and the connection is freely flowing between a regulated parent and a dysregulated child, any amount of stress coming from the child is within capacity. Of course, the keyword here is "regulated" parent. As long as this dynamic stays in tact, the sky's the limit.

When we can stay regulated during our children's most difficult moments, we are equipping them with "experiential knowledge." This is knowledge gained through experience. They are learning how to shift back to a state of regulation through their experiences with us. This equips them to be able to do this on their own, hence they are developing their self-regulatory abilities to later enter into the "real world." The more we can equip our children now, the more they will have the capacity to stay regulated on their own in a dysregulated and stressed out world.

■

The more we can equip our children now, the more they will have the capacity to stay regulated on their own in a dysregulated and stressed out world.

■

Social Outings

Q: *How can I help prepare my child for social situations like a trip to the dentist or getting a haircut? He becomes so defiant and when I finally do get him there, it typically turns into a disaster. So, my next question is, how can I handle the situation effectively when it does not go so well?*

A: In order to prepare children for social situations like going to the dentist or getting a haircut, it is important to realize that the underlying issue behind the resistance is fear. When parents can address the child's fear, and calm their child's stress, these situations do not have to be such hurdles anymore. Simply seeing a child as a scared child as opposed to a resistant child, allows the parent to provide safety and reassurance at an entirely new level.

Work to calm your child before you even leave the house. Sit with your child, physically touch him through an embrace or a touch on the arm or shoulder. Then talk with your child. Being attuned from the child's emotional perspective, not an adult perspective, is a key task. We tend to rationalize, minimize, and normalize our children's fear saying, "Oh, it won't be so bad, don't worry." Instead, if the child's fears are truly heard and the parent can validate those fears, without feeling like they have to convince the child of feeling differently, the child will then have the emotional space to find his own courage and feel secure enough in the parent/child relationship to move forward.

If you have done everything to help your child at an emotional level and he still continues to be unable to move through these situations in an appropriate way, it is not a reflection of you. Too many times parents take this personally. They are embarrassed by their child's behavior and they invalidate themselves as parents based on the child's inability to respond to the parent's efforts. The reality is that it is not about the parent. It is simply about the child not being ready. Ironically, the more the parent can give the child emotional space and accept the child's lack of readiness, the more the child will be able to work through these situations in the future.

Ironically, the more the parent can give the child emotional space and accept the child's lack of readiness, the more the child will be able to work through these situations in the future.

Adding more stress to your child through well intended parenting strategies such as incentives and rewards can actually be detrimental. An already stressed out child may not be able to handle the stress of receiving or not receiving a reward. We need to respect our children's natural path of development and healing. Respecting our children in the present, realizing that they will find their way with parental acceptance, love, and support around them, is essential. Given this, children learn they are perfectly acceptable and unconditionally loved. This is what provides the safety for them to then take the next steps in their development, not external rewards or incentives. When we work to connect and support our children, they will not be 18 years old and still scared to get a haircut. And more importantly, they will not have bad memories of relational disconnect with their parents around such events.

Q: *What do we do when dysregulation occurs in another environment (outside the home) and we (the parents) are there? We realize it is an overstimulating environment, but a common environment he will be in and needs to learn how to regulate in it.*

A: I want to first address the fear I hear in this question. I hear the parent being worried that her child will not be able to regulate in this environment, not just now – but ever! This fear of the future causes us to lose sight of where we are in the present and it paints a bleak picture of the future with our children. In between the lines, I hear the parent saying, "But if Johnny doesn't develop the ability to go to the grocery store, he'll never be able to be on his own and be a responsible adult. I'll have to shop for him until he is 35 years old!" Rightfully so, it is a parent's deepest desire to help her child grow up to be a responsible and well functioning adult.

Yet, the only way to equip our children is to teach them the skills and help them stay regulated, without pushing them and forcing them beyond their developmental capacities. It takes meeting the child exactly where he is in the present moment. It requires the parent owning his fear instead of projecting it onto the child (which will only make the situation more stressful). Let us take the example of helping Johnny make it through the grocery store, a task he certainly will need to be able to handle as an adult. Here are some suggestions to make these trips successful:

■

It requires the parent owning his fear instead of projecting it onto the child.

■

Prior to leaving the house, the parent can set aside time to connect with the child. Sit on the couch with Johnny and talk with him about the upcoming trip to the store, focusing on how the parent is going to be there to create safety and security. The conversation might look something like this:

"Johnny, we are going to leave in about 10 minutes to go to the grocery store. *(Parent breathes and works to calm down because just the thought of going to the grocery store fires up the parent's amygdala and the parent begins to shift into a fear state.)* I know that the store is a hard place to be and you may not always feel safe. I haven't understood this in the past, so I want to help make this trip better for the both of us. I want you to stay near me and perhaps you might even feel safer by sitting in the shopping cart *(of course this is to be adjusted depending on the child's size and age)* or holding onto the cart with me. At any time, if you start to feel scared or overwhelmed, I want you to tell me so I can help you. If it ever becomes too much, it is okay. We'll simply leave the store so you can be okay. Nothing I can buy at the store is more important than you feeling safe and calm."

When you get into the car and leave for the store, play calming music and open up the conversation with your child – anything that he will be open to talking about. Too many times we use this driving time to return phone calls while our child pulls out his Gameboy to keep himself occupied.

When you pull up in the parking lot, take a few extra minutes to relax. Go over the list. Talk about what you will be buying. If like most children, your child has always found toys, candy, or other items he wants you to buy for him, let him know that you understand how hard it is for him when you say no to these requests. Give him permission to be upset that he can not have everything he wants. Validate him and tell him you also have a hard time not buying everything you want and desire. Tell him again what you told him before you left the house, reassuring him that you are there to help him through this trip to the store and that he is not alone.

> ■
>
> *You can only expect your child to be as regulated as you are.*
>
> ■

Have him join you in the shopping by holding the list, looking for bargains, or in some way engaging him in this experience. Check in with him periodically while you are in the store together. And more importantly, check in with yourself to make sure you are truly regulated in order for him to work off of your regulation. Remember that you can only expect your child to be as regulated as you are.

The more positive experiences you can create in the present, the more your child will be able to handle overstimulating environments in the future. It takes baby steps sometimes. Be patient and enjoy the responsibility you have been given to prepare your child for a wonderful future. Trust in the process.

Hitting, Kicking, Biting, Talking

Q: *We have been in the trenches with our eight-year-old nephew. I have tried to talk to him with words of empathy and understanding, saying them passionately. Yet, he will not allow us to talk. He puts his fingers in his ears and yells over our voices. Even when he is calm he will not allow any talk about his feelings. Yesterday when he was out* *of control throwing objects at me, hitting and kicking me, he screamed through tears, "I am going to treat you just like my Mama treated me!!!" I said, "tell me about it, how did it make you feel?" He said, "scared, but now I found out that it's fun and I am going to do it to you. It doesn't scare me when I'm the one doing it." He did not slow down the attack at all. This is one of the few times he talked, but only because he was so into his attack that he could not put his fingers in his ears. How can we reach him?*

A: I realize your nephew continued to throw objects, yet a huge smile covered my face when I first read your question. You did reach your nephew. Plus, you reached him in the midst of his emotional reaction. *Celebrate this victory!*

Your nephew was able to make a connection with you and you were able to interrupt the negative feedback loop that has been a part of your past experiences with him. *Celebrate this victory!*

You gained a new understanding of why he is aggressive and angry. He told you exactly why he acts this way. You now know that he is intensely angry at his mom. *Celebrate this victory!*

You now have the permission to not take his behavior personally. He is not angry at you; he is angry at his mother. *Celebrate this victory!*

The fear from his past experiences was identified when you asked him how it made him feel when his mom was mean to him. He said, "Scared." He is in touch with his fear. *Celebrate this victory!*

■

Love is letting go of the fear.

■

You stated that this was one of the few times he talked during his behavioral outbursts, an interruption of the pattern occurred. *Celebrate this victory!*

I could keep pointing out all the positive pieces to celebrate in this interaction with your nephew because what you were able to do with him was a huge accomplishment. We often stay so focused on the outcome that we miss the moments of victory. These moments may seem small, momentary, and even insignificant, but they are the first steps forward in the healing and connection process. You cannot expect to run a marathon the day after you decide to get back into a physical fitness program after being a couch potato. Running around the block without passing out may be the first step in your marathon goal.

Love is letting go of the fear. Fear says that we have to fix it right now, right away, and right on time. Fear keeps us from celebrating the monumental first steps towards healing. Step back . . . breathe and focus on the positive.

I know you want more concrete answers to this aggression piece. I know first hand what it is like to have a son literally beating up on you and scaring the life out of you. I will never minimize this.

Safety is always first. But I want you to realize that 95% of the time, we, the parents, are the ones who turn a disruptive situation into an unsafe situation. If you have to leave to get yourself out of harms way, let him know that you are not going far, that you will never leave him like other people have left him, but that you are simply making it safe for him and for you.

95% of the time, we, the parents, are the ones who turn a disruptive situation into an unsafe situation.

Recognize that your nephew was throwing the objects because he was seeking safety and seeking to reduce his fear. He said, "It doesn't scare me when I'm the one doing it." Your dialogue and relational connection with him has a thousand times more potential for creating safety for him . . . he just does not have the blueprint for that at this time.

I would suspect that you became scared when he replied, ". . . but now I found out that it's fun and I am going to do it to you." When children laugh or define fun from hurtful acts, we often hear this and slide into our fear patterns, "Oh my gosh, he thinks it is fun to hurt – he is going to grow up to be the next Ted Bundy!" The reality is that when our fear becomes too overwhelming, we easily shift into the opposite feeling state. Have you ever laughed or smirked when you were nervous or scared about something? I am certain you can think of at least two examples of this.

Meet your nephew right in the center of his conversation. When he said it was fun, you could reply by saying, "I bet it is fun. You finally feel safe and in control, don't you?" Validate him. Accept him. Acknowledge him. Apologize to him. "I'm so sorry you were treated so poorly. I wish I could have been there to keep you safe. I'm so sorry I wasn't there to help you." Allow yourself to cry, if you feel yourself welling up with tears. You are sad that he went through these experiences. Let your passion overflow so he knows how loved he is. "I love you so much. I never would have let this happen to you."

This type of continuing conversation to meet him in his emotional state has the power to stop his attack. He was not able to slow down be-cause it appears that once he said it was fun, you froze and became over-whelmed in fear yourself. Take the next step forward with him, staying attuned to what he is saying. Remember that it is not about you. Your fear has to be set aside in the moment so you can connect with him in the depths of his terror. He needs you to join him in this space.

It is about love, understanding, acceptance, patience, and the willingness to jump into our children's pain with them. **These moments "in the raw" are the openings for deep and permanent healing.** That is love – setting aside yourself to be an instrument of peace and regulation for your child.

Q: *Our seven-year-old grandson (who we are raising) exhibits constant talking, questioning, arguing, lying for attention, and interrupting. It seems totally connected to his abandonment and neglect history. How do we diffuse it?*

A: You are right on the mark. These behaviors are being driven from past experiences of being left, ignored, and abandoned. Your grandson is in survival mode, making certain this time around he is not going to be invisible and that he will indeed exist.

The communication screaming out in these behaviors is, "I need you to know that I exist! I need you to connect with me so I don't disappear and die! Hear me! See me! Talk to me! Give me attention. Acknowledge me. Make connection with me so I know I'll be okay!" His chronic fear of being abandoned and neglected is driving all these "annoying" behaviors.

I use quotes around the word annoying because these behaviors are only annoying if we do not understand why he is acting this way. If we truly understand how terrified he is, these behaviors will only move us closer to him and draw us to relate to his needs.

> ■
>
> *Children act out because they need attention.*
>
> ■

Children act out because they need attention. Unfortunately, this acting out has been interpreted by many professionals as children being manipulative and "bratty." If you were to react to these behaviors under this false interpretation, you would simply be creating more of the same – more fear, and more pain. Rejecting him through consequences would only heighten his sense of not being important to those around him.

In order to extinguish these behaviors, you must soothe the internal fear. When he is chattering or questioning, refrain from the surface conversation and give him words to calm the storm brewing inside of him. Put your arm around him and say, "I love you. I'm so glad you're in my life. You're so special to me." Continue to respond to him throughout the day with words that will create security and calm his fears ("You bring happiness into my day." "I'm here for you always." "I'm so glad I get to take care of you!").

Every child on this planet has an innate need to feel special (just as we do as adults!). Being special to someone ensures our survival. Link yourself in a close relationship with your grandson and you will help him shift out of survival, into a secure place to finally be a playful child. As your relationship deepens and he experiences you at a whole new level, the behaviors he is using to create this security on his own will disappear.

Q: *My child refuses to participate in family activities. For example, I can say, "Let's go on a family hike." He'll say, "No! You know I hate hiking. You can't make me!" How should I respond?*

A: One of the best ways to connect with someone is to meet him where his is. This is a universal rule for connecting with anyone, whether it be a coworker, friend, or stranger at a party. It takes showing genuine interest in the other person's desires, interests, and dreams.

If we feel as if nobody cares about us, it is difficult to get outside our own needs and interests in order to meet other people's needs. Your son needs you to connect with him solely, in his little corner of the universe. It is not that he won't participate in family activities, it is simply that he can't right now.

Listen to the words your child is using: "No. You know I hate hiking." He is saying, "Nobody gets me! Nobody respects what I like to do and you're all too busy trying to get me to do what you want to do!" Herein lies the answer.

Be intentional about making a date with just him and you. Ask him what he would like to do. Let him plan the day. Tell him that what he likes to do is important to you and you want to be able to do it with him.

Once he feels like his needs are understood and he is important enough for you to take an entire day or afternoon to play in his world, he will have the capacity to participate in the larger family activities. Like every child, he needs to feel special, unique, and important. Then, he will be energized to be an active and happy participant with everybody.

Q: *My daughter, now six years old, is hitting herself in the face. It is happening constantly. We have consulted with a psychologist and have her on a "sticker chart" broken down into time increments where she gets a reward when she is not hitting. But, so far, it is not working. I mentioned to my psychologist that my daughter has a history of medical issues that were quite extensive, but he said that would not have had an effect on her because she was only an infant at the time.*

A: Your daughter's issues are far deeper than the behavior you are seeing at the surface. A sticker chart, while recommended by a good-intentioned professional, is like putting a Band-aid on the chest of someone who is bleeding internally. It will have absolutely no effect.

Behavior modification techniques, such as sticker charts, rewards systems, and token economies, only address the behavior, not what is going on internally within the child. They deal with only the symptoms. To effectively help a child, it takes looking at all the different levels of the child's make-up. These include behavioral, cognitive, emotional, psychological, social, and physical levels.

Children who are given the message early in life that, "I am not wanted," "I am not loved," and/or "I am not lovable," find themselves in a place of internal conflict. Medical trauma, where there is intense pain and isolation for a child, can create these negative messages in a child, especially when the child is an infant. These experiences of overwhelm to the nervous system both emotionally and physically, can have a tremendous effect on a child's development and state of internal regulation.

Due to these early experiences, your daughter is in a state of fear and hyper-sensitivity. Some children react against others, becoming aggressive and defiant towards their caretakers, while other children turn against themselves, banging their heads and causing self-harm.

Your daughter is trying to calm her internal state of stress and dysregulation by slapping her face. She is living in an internal state of heightened stress. This is simply her attempt at calming down her nervous system that is firing in hyper-drive.

The other core issue is self-rejection. Medical trauma leaves infants and children feeling like they are not lovable and they must be bad (Why else would these painful things be happening to them?). A child's mind is egocentric and when bad things happen, the interpretation is that it must be their fault.

It is interesting to note that this problem of self-rejection is actually one of the most universal and least recognized issues in our society and is the root of most of our relationship issues. It is what keeps us from being able to give or receive love freely. It would be a good exercise for you to check in with yourself on this issue of self-rejection. We all reject or hate some part of ourselves, often without being consciously aware of it. Stay cognizant of how her self-rejection issues might be affecting you.

The solution comes in your daughter learning to love herself and learning to be comforted, soothed, and loved through her relationship with you. The best way she can learn this is from her primary caregiver – you. Her internal program is engraved with messages of rejection, abandonment, and being unlovable.

Rewriting this blueprint and repatterning her nervous system becomes your challenging task. As a parent who was once faced with this same responsibility, I can honestly say that there is no other task more difficult on this planet. The message you will be giving her is in direct contradiction to her internal working models.

Accepting these new messages of "You are lovable." and "I'm here to calm and soothe you." within her psyche will take patience, tolerance, understanding, acceptance, and repetition. In short, it will take unconditional love. She will reject this message, reject herself, and reject the world around her as she works through this realigning process.

In order to help your daughter through this process, here are a few suggestions. Safety for your daughter will be the first place to start. When she starts hitting herself in the face, see if she will allow you to hold her, even rock her. She has disrupted early life experiences of being effectively regulated through her "upsets." She needs your help in learning how to calm her system down effectively. This will eliminate the need to hit herself.

Lovingly tell her that it is your responsibility, as her parent, to keep her safe and calm. Let her know it is your job to make sure she does not hurt herself. See if she can hold your hand, squeeze it as hard as she can, instead of slapping herself. Do not restrain her hands as this will only cause more stress. If she insists on slapping her face, simply put a pillow in between her hand and her face, preventing her from harming herself.

Begin to give her the story of what happened when she was a baby. Talk to her about how painful it must have been for her and that while you were there with her as much as you could be, you were not able to take her pain away. Explain that she was probably very scared and feeling all alone. Express your grief and apologize for how difficult it must have been for her. Children are exceptionally tangible and concrete thinkers, so you might want to tell her this story through stuffed animals or dolls.

Work to secure her foundation with you so that she can learn how to regulate herself through you. Create more opportunities for attachment and bonding. Below is a general list of suggested activities for creating secure attachments. Pick a few that are appropriate and be intentional about making time for them:

Rocking	Swimming
Feeding	Having Fun (JOY!)
Bottle Feeding	Spending Time Together
Talking	Creating a Life Book
Playing	Giving Your Child Her Story
Hugging	Playing "Hide and Seek"
Massage / Touch	Tickling
Cuddling	Wrestling
	Co-Bathing (age appropriate)

Remember, stickers are for fun and not the solution themselves. A million stickers could never substitute a relationship with you.

Breathing

Q: *Do you have any techniques for teaching a child to take deep breaths? I've tried to use this with my son and he just breathes faster and it makes him more dysregulated.*

A: For younger children, pick up a bottle of bubbles at your local dollar store. This is a great way to visually see how breathing can create something magnificent. Have fun blowing bubbles together and teach your child how to blow super big bubbles by breathing slowly and precisely. Too heavy a breath will burst the bubble, so this is a great way to teach a child intentional deep breathing.

For older children (and this works with younger children as well), there is a device called a pulse oximeter, also referred to as a pulse ox. It measures the oxygen level in your body by attaching to your index finger. The mechanism uses light at two different wavelengths. The absorption of this light between the top of the finger and bottom of the finger is measured. (The amount of light absorbed depends on the saturation level of oxygen in the blood's hemoglobin). By calculating the absorption at the two wavelengths, the processor can compute the proportion of hemoglobin that is oxygenated, giving you a reading of your oxygen level. As you breathe, you can see the number on the digital monitor increase, which is an indication of your oxygen level increasing. It is lots of fun to have a child watch the effects of breathing on his body. These devices are a bit expensive, but if you are resourceful, you may be able to find a nurse or doctor who has one. or bid on one through eBay. Even if you only use it once, it gives children a visual representation of how breathing affects the body's system that can leave a lasting imprint.

For children who are inquisitive, do some research on the effects of oxygen on the body. Teach your child that there are three ways to influence a person's nervous system. These include glucose (food), input (exercise), and oxygen. Of these three, the most effective is oxygen. For children who are super inquisitive and always wanting to know "why," look up the different air qualities in cities around the globe. Historically, the oxygen content in the air was about 35%, but most cities today run about 20%. Larger polluted cities can be as low as 12%. The point is to meet your child at his level of interest in order to teach him how to do something, like breathing, that may not initially interest him.

You can also work with your child to count during breathing. Play with this at first and see how long you can each last on the inhale, counting up as high as you can before feeling like you are going to burst. Then do the same for the exhale. He will love being able to out number his parent. Remember that play is a child's language. Have fun with it during the calm moments and you will be able to help him shift out of the dysregulated moments by introducing the same playful techniques.

Attitude

Q: *Should I care about the attitude my child exhibits when she is asked to pick up her room (i.e. stomping up the stairs, talking back, etc.)?*

A: Initially, I believe it is important to first learn how to accept your child with the behaviors she is exhibiting. This is the biggest challenge of all. Once you get past this, you will understand how to address the behaviors in an accepting and loving way with her. As a parent you must first accept her exactly, fully, and completely, however she is acting. To do this we must go back to the understanding that behavior is not an act or a target towards us personally.

Behavior is a form of communication. It is a form of communication for a child who is dysregulated and who has moved from a state of love to a state of fear and overwhelm. When we can wrap our brain around this and understand that when our child starts stomping up the stairs or begins to talk back after we have asked her to do something, then what we can see is a child who is simply overwhelmed. This allows us to see that in front of us is a child who does not know how to behave in the moment because underneath it she is too stressed out. This is a cry for relationship.

So the question is, "Should I care about the attitude?" Yes, you should care, but in a different way. You should care because what she is telling you is that she is stressed out.

I encourage you to join her in this state of distress and acknowledge that she is doing what you asked her to do. "Honey, thank you for coming upstairs to clean your room. I know it is hard to do such a big task." All too often we not only expect our children to be obedient and compliant, but we expect them to do it with a smile and gratitude for us being their parents. Acknowledge the positive, yet acknowledge her overwhelm, as well. Ignore the attitude until later.

We as adults have to do things we don't want to do. For me, I hate grocery shopping. Yet, I do it because it needs to get done. I have learned to find ways to make it more enjoyable, like going when it is less crowded, seeing how fast I can make it in and out of the store and timing myself to the second, and staying focused on why I am there (to be the best parent I can be and to provide for my children's needs).

Teach your daughter how to make chores fun. Join her and play basketball with the clothes and the hamper. Have a pillow fight in between picking up the toys. Play loud music and dance together. The key to attachment is joy. Shift these moments of negativity into joyful moments focused on the relationship you are building with her. (See *Beyond Consequences, Logic, and Control, Volume 2,* for more on the issue of chores).

Once you are both connected, talk to her about how to express herself in a more loving way, instead of using attitude. Give her permission to come ask you for help or to just vent that she does not like to clean her room. The next time she vents and says, "I don't like to clean my room," you can validate her by saying, "I know. It's not much fun just to clean, is it? What can you do to make it fun?" Empower her to make life situations different. She has the ability to make her life work for her and you have the opportunity to show her how to do that. Plus, you might want to join her again for a good game of shooting laundry into the hamper!

Resistance

Q: *My husband and I are baffled by our daughter, age nine-and-a-half, who still has some really bad days, even after implementing the techniques in Beyond Consequences, Logic, and Control. Here are a few examples:*

Scenario 1:
Mom: "It's time to put clothes on *(that we have laid out the night before).*
Daughter: "I'm too cold . . . I'm too tired . . . I don't want to wear those . . . those don't fit . . . they give me wedgies." *(She goes limp, starts crying)* "I can't . . . I'm not going to."

Scenario 2:
Mom: "It's bedtime."
Daughter: *(She goes limp)* "I'm too tired" *(She curls up into a ball on the floor and starts crying).*

Scenario 3:
Dad: "Let's have a nice dinner and go out to ABC."
Daughter: "I only want to eat at XXX *(There is only one restaurant she likes).* "It's not fair . . . you always get to pick. I never get to have

what I want." *(She starts crying and drops to the floor)*.

We try to spending time together. We try the *"Sounds like you are really tired and you don't want to wear those, etc."* response. I ask her if I can just hold her, give her a hug, and sometimes that works. I ask her if I can feed her, and sometimes that works. I ask her what is she afraid of and sometimes if I help her with the possibilities, that works. But I still feel so hopeless sometimes.

A: Implementing the *Beyond Consequences* model can be difficult in the midst of stress, frustration, and overwhelm. Your daughter is presenting situations that feel as if she is being defiant, resistant, and illogical. And you are left feeling powerless and hopeless, baffled by her behaviors.

> ■
>
> *The reality is that your child's behaviors are quite logical from her point of view.*
>
> ■

When we are baffled by our child's behaviors, we have to step back and ask ourselves one question, "Who defines the logic?" If we cannot see the logic from our child's perspective it will leave us baffled and frustrated.

The reality is that your child's behaviors are quite logical from her point of view. Her frame of reference is simply different from yours. So, the answers lie in understanding your child's perspective and seeking to connect with the fear that is driving her behaviors.

Looking at Scenario 1, we see from the adult perspective that we have taken the time the night before to lay out her clothes, giving her predictability, avoiding too many choices in the morning, and helping her get dressed. All of these are great.

However, I would guess that this is a weekday morning and time to go to school and leave the house. From your daughter's perspective, those clothes lying in front of her resemble a day of stress, uncertainty, and distance from you. Depending on her history, she may very well see those clothes as a one-way ticket from home, without a guarantee that she will come home in the afternoon. Our thoughts become our reality. This being her reality, of course she refuses to put on these clothes.

Her resistance is the communication of her fear, no matter how distorted it may seem to us as adults. It will take meeting her in this reality to help her see a new perspective and calm her stress. Giving her logic and reasoning from a cognitive place will not override the core emotional interpretation of the situation.

Continuing the script, we can develop the dialogue:

Scenario 1:

Mom: "It's time to put clothes on *(that we have laid out the night before).*

Daughter: "I'm too cold . . . I'm too tired . . . I don't want to wear those . . . Those don't fit . . . They give me wedgies." *(She goes limp, starts crying)* "I can't . . . I'm not going to."

Mom: *(Realizes that her daughter's resistance is fear and simply sits down on the bed and takes a deep breath, not saying a word. She reaches out her arms, offering a hug.)*

Daughter: *(Refuses to acknowledge the gesture as love).* "Stop. I hate you."

Mom: *(Shifting her perspective, mom reaches inside herself to see that her daughter is not rejecting her but her daughter is rejecting herself).* "I love you and I'm never leaving you. I am here to help you work through this."

Daughter: "Leave me alone."

Mom: *(Meeting her daughter's request instead of jumping into a control battle, Mom realizes that her daughter is overwhelmed by the unconditional love being expressed. Her daughter fears rejection, so she works to reject her mother first in order to protect herself. Her daughter is living in a place of emotional survival.)* "Sometimes it can be scary to have someone simply love you and trust that they are not going to leave you or hurt you. I understand that."

Daughter: "No you don't."

Mom: "Well, you're absolutely right. I don't understand it as well as you. *(Relates in her mind that in her own childhood she didn't experience the same trauma as her daughter).* Would you help me understand? I want to know what it is like for you.

Daughter: "I don't want to go to school. I don't want to wear those clothes. I don't even want you to touch me. I hate you. I hate my life and I hate everybody and everybody hates me."

Instead of saying such statements as, "Well that's not true, not everybody hates you, honey," or "These were the clothes that you picked out last night, so that's what you need to wear today," Mom shifts to a place of validating her daughter's perspective. Mom knows that as her daughter's stress calms down, Mom will have a chance to affirm her daughter's worth but if she does this now, her daughter will continue to resist her. Her daughter simply needs emotional space at this moment to process through all this negativity.

Mom then continues to let her daughter take the lead in the conversa-

tion, accepting that her daughter already has the ability within herself to find her way out of this. Her daughter needs unconditional love, support, validation, acceptance, and patience in order to make this journey to healing.

Scenario 2

The directive of bedtime puts your daughter into a state of complete overwhelm. At this point in the day, she is too tired to even think about getting up and walking into her bedroom. It may feel like walking 10 miles uphill to make it to that bedroom. Her nervous system is exhausted from her day of living in survival.

Have you ever been so sick with the flu that even getting up to get yourself something to drink feels like a monumental task? This is the same sensation that your daughter goes through when she cries and curls up in a ball on the floor. Use your experiences of the past to connect with her frame of reference in the present moment. When you are weak from the flu, what do you need? You need someone to do it for you until you can regain your strength. Let us complete this dialogue from Scenario 2:

Mom: "It's bedtime."
Daughter: *(She goes limp)* "I'm too tired" *(She curls up into a ball on the floor and starts crying).*
Mom: "I've got you, sweetheart." *(Mom bends down to pick up her daughter or if she is too heavy, asks Dad to help.)* You've had a hard day and I'm just glad you're home with us now so we can help you through this.

The fear in us says, "If I help her tonight, then every night she is going to continue this 'manipulative' behavior." This fear response comes from the old view that says we will be reinforcing the negative behavior if we respond to it. The truth is that children act out or 'manipulate' because they need attention. By responding to her, while ignoring the behavior, the mom will be working to calm her daughter's physiological system that is depleted and overwhelmed. As her daughter shifts out of survival and begins to recognize love as safety, mom will see a child that can handle simple parental directives. As mom works through these scenarios in the future, she can work to teach her daughter how to ask for help appropriately instead of falling into a big puddle of emotional protoplasm. Mom will see a child who then has the tools to ask for help and can verbally express her needs without going to extremes.

Scenario 3

Here we find dad wanting to do something nice yet he receives resistance and whining from his daughter. Unconditional love means to put something out to someone without any expectations or conditions, which would give dad permission to meet the daughter in her resistance instead of resisting her resistance with more resistance.

Dad: "Let's have a nice dinner and go out to ABC."

Daughter: "I want to eat at xxx. It's not fair . . . you always get to pick. I never get to have what I want." *(She starts crying and drops to the floor).*

Dad: *(Gives himself permission to step out of the authoritative dad position and recognizes that his daughter is expressing a deeper issue of not feeling special, not feeling alright, and not feeling worthy).* You're really upset, aren't you?

Daughter: *(She continues to cry even harder).*

Dad: *(Recognizing that even though the crying intensified, this does not mean that the daughter is getting 'her' way as Dad would had previously thought. Dad now sees that he has made a connection with his daughter and continues to work to enhance this connection with her.)* It feels like you never get to have what you want, doesn't it?

Daughter: I don't! You do whatever you want without EVER asking me!

Dad: That must make you feel really unimportant. I must not be doing my part to make sure you know how important you are to me. Can you sit up here with me? *(Offers his lap and open arms).*

Daughter: *(ignores Dad and keeps crying).*

Dad: *(Dad recognizes that she is simply too engulfed in her fear and overwhelm to get up to meet him, so he joins her on the floor. He rubs her back and whispers in a soft tone.)* You're the apple of my eye, sunshine, and I'm so lucky to have you as my daughter.

Daughter: *Daughter curls up closer to dad but still doesn't acknowledge him with her eyes or words.*

Dad: *(Dad works to keep himself regulated so that his daughter can feel his calm presence. Dad realizes that you cannot meet resistance with more resistance and make the situation better. He breaths; he reminds himself that this whole scenario unfolded from her lack of self-worth, not from his inability to be an effective parent. So he invites her in again and shifts her onto his lap and just holds her.)*

You cannot meet resistance with more resistance and make the situation better.

Daughter: *(Takes a deep breath and begins to settle down).*
Dad: I love you.

... after a few minutes of just connecting and settling down, Dad can work to shift the interaction back to the beginning, helping to support her in going out to dinner.

Dad: "I realize you want to go to xxx for dinner and you may still be upset that we're not going there tonight. You can be upset and I want you to know that I can handle your feelings. I want to keep you close to me just like we are now and I was wondering if it would be okay for us to sit together when we're there? You're too special to me for me not to help you through the hard times in life."

> ■
> *Every interaction with your child is an opportunity for growth, healing, and deeper connection.*
> ■

Every interaction with your child is an opportunity for growth, healing, and deeper connection. Reacting from a place of frustration, helplessness, and stress only creates more of the same. Embrace these interactions, rise above behaviors, and connect with the special child within through unconditional love, acceptance, and understanding. Shift your perspective and the behaviors that were once baffling will suddenly make perfect sense.

Q: *How do you deal with a child who does not open up. When asked, "What are you feeling?", he responds, "Never mind. Nothing."*

A: When a child responds like this, in a minimizing and avoiding way, it is indicative of a child who could be feeling one of several of the following ways:

- "I really don't matter to her. I'm worth nothing."
- "She can't handle what I'm saying. She might get mad or upset at me."
- "I dare not let anyone know how I feel ... they'll not love me anymore."
- "I shouldn't be feeling this way. I'm stupid."
- "Whatever! She won't 'get' me. Nobody gets me."
- "I'm scared. Okay, I'm terrified of not being good enough."
- "If I tell you, you'll stop loving me."

Instead of facing one or any of the above thoughts, it is easier for your child to simply shut down and disconnect, both from himself and from you. Pushing your child to open up and tell you at this point will only threaten him more. The more you push, the more he will avoid. If you try to get a turtle to come out of his shell and you start tapping on his shell, you are sure to prevent him from coming out for an extended period of time.

This is the time to step back, acknowledge how difficult it must be to talk about it, and then offer to be available when your child is ready. You will be giving your child "emotional space." Emotional space entails first validating your child, then allowing him the time to process through his fear. Reassure your child that you love him and that you are available if he needs you.

Humor can sometimes create an atmosphere of safety and security. Here is a game you might try with your son, or any child who is too fearful to discuss what is going on in his or her life. It is called "Two Truths and a Lie." You invite your child to talk about three things about his life, two of which are actual truths and one that is not. You have to guess which one is the "lie." If he is resistant to starting out the game, offer to go first. You might have to go a few times in a row before he will be able to take a turn. Pick some topics in your life that have a moderate level of emotional content, so it matches his level of emotional distress.

You will be modeling for him the act of being vulnerable. You will be showing him you trust him enough to share your feelings. You will also give him the opportunity to see that your life is not perfect and that having feelings and frustrations is acceptable in your household.

This is also a game that can be played at the dinner table with the whole family as a way to engage each other in a conversation about the day's activities. Each child gets a chance at the game. This gives each child a chance to be heard, to feel important, and to have an opportunity to be a part of the entire family system. You will find that this will also open up communication to more issues going on in your child's life.

Incessant Chatter

Q: *How do you deal with a child who asks over 100 questions a day?*

A: When a child is constantly asking questions, he is needing to know the future, that he is going to be okay, and that you have not forgotten about him. These questions are being driven from a need to be safe and secure. Responding back with reason and logic can prove futile.

Brain science is showing us that our ability to comprehend logic, reasoning, and planning resides in the third brain, the neocortex. For the child in this question, the constant barrage of questions indicates that he is living in survival, disconnected from this place of higher level thinking. All the logic and reasoning you provide him will mean absolutely nothing in the moment.

I am certain that the asking and the asking and the asking, over and over and over again, puts you in a place of low tolerance. You then shift from being patient to becoming stressed and inpatient. Your child senses this from within you, becomes more fearful, and BOOM! The exact fear of being rejected and unwanted is then being created right in the midst of him trying to get reassurance from you. More of the same has just been experienced for your child and your child, in using the only coping mechanism he has, begins to ask more questions!

When it comes to survival, remember that there is no prize for second place, hence, the relentlessness of questions. It is your child's way of ensuring his survival, at all costs. He is thinking, "I must know what we are doing next. I must know that I'm alright. I must know that I'm safe." Logical thinking will not calm him because these questions are being driven from an emotional place.

In order to calm him and create safety, it is going to take connecting with him at an emotional level. Blocked feelings need to be released in order to help him shift out of this place of survival. Effectively interrupting this cycling of questions cannot come from verbal answers, even though that is what appears to be what he is seeking. These questions are being driven from fear. Connecting with the fear is the solution.

It will take you seeing this fully in order to not continually be feeding him logical answers. "Dance" with his emotional state behind the questions. Here is an example of a dialogue that could develop when he starts asking his questions:

Son: "Where are we going now?"
Mom: "We are going to the grocery store and then we'll be stopping off at Grandma's."
Son: "Why are we going to Grandma's?"
Mom: (now sensing that they are getting back into the all too familiar loop) "I love you and I want to let you know that I'm here to take care of you so you are safe."
Son: "But why are we going to Grandma's?"
Mom: "Is there something that scares you about going to Grandma's?"
Son: "She's old."
Mom: (Puts the reactive response of, "That's not nice to say" on the back burner.) "Yes, she is old" (validating her son).
Son: "I don't like to go to Grandma's."

Mom: *(Again, resists the typical rational response of: "Well, we have to go to Grandma's and I expect you to be nice to her while we are there.")* "What is it about Grandma's that scares you?"

Son: "She might die."

Mom: "Wow! That is scary. Dying can be a scary thing."

Son: "What if you die?"

Mom: *(First reaction to downplay this question by saying, "I'm not going to die" is halted).* "That is a scary thought, isn't it?"

> ■
> *Instead of scratching the surface of what you are hearing, open the door to what your child is feeling.*
> ■

The conversation shifts from an irritating tennis match of dialogue to one of in-depth emotional exploration. Instead of scratching the surface of what you are hearing, open the door to what your child is feeling. Unleash the fear through your relationship and through your ability to take on the full extent of what is going on beneath your child's surface. Remember that love-based parenting elevates your concern for the mundane to that of deeper connection and emotional healing.

Disrespect

Q: *My adopted son, now 13 years old, was in a dysregulated home in his early years. He is so arrogant and disrespectful to me and his father at times. I have recognized that this behavior increases when he is stressed out but I'm just not sure I am teaching him how to be respectful. I'm worried that when he grows up and gets stressed out on the job, he'll disrespect his boss and get fired.*

A: It has been said that 95% of what children learn is from what is modeled to them. They are like mirrors, reflecting back what adults say and do.

I would suspect that during your son's early years, prior to coming home to you and your husband, he saw others behaving this way and/or he was treated this way. It is likely that the intensity of these behaviors also increased during times of stress.

Humans, especially children, absorb everything that we experience. The mind absorbs everything at a subconscious level. If we do not have the appropriate filters operating (which children do not), we get programmed (see *Beyond Consequences, Logic, and Control, Volume 2*). The adults in your child's early life were role models (negative role models are still role models). This is such a prime example of what we grow up hearing is the language we will speak.

In times of stress, the first two parts of our brain are activated. The third brain, the neocortex, our thinking brain, is dormant. This means that we cannot learn, we only record. Your son was only recording what was being modeled during his early years.

These old patterns, however, do not have to be lifelong. Your son has the ability to learn new ways of interacting through your modeling of love by giving him respect, tolerance, patience, and understanding. Doing this during times of being disrespected by him requires intention, commitment, and mindfulness on your part.

During these difficult moments, stay in a place of awareness of how brain plasticity is working to correct this negative disrespectful programming. In its most basic definition, the brain's ability to reorganize neural pathways is called neuroplasticity. The study of neuroplasticity is perhaps the single most exciting area of brain-related research that has exploded in science today.

The brain is constantly creating new areas and new connections, rerouting existing connections, morphing and undulating in response to new information. In the mid-1990's research by Tortora & Grabowski showed that when learning new information, there are actually two distinct changes occurring in our brains. First, there is a change in the internal structure of the neurons themselves, specifically in the area of synapses. Second, there is an increase in the number of synapses between neurons.

This information means that your son, when experiencing respect from you in response to his dysregulation and disrespect, will experience new growth in his brain (synapses and neuron changes). You are literally repatterning his neurological system in these moments.

How you treat your child is how you teach your child.

Giving this respect also requires you to look closely at some of your patterned responses. Ask yourself, "Would I reply in the same way to my best friend as I just did with my child?" This can be a genuine gauge as to the level of respect you truly are demonstrating to your child.

Many of our responses are simply "old tapes" from our own childhood. Would you say, "What's the magic word?" or "What do you say?" to your best friend? If you want your children to say please and thank you on a consistent basis, it will require you demonstrating it to them first.

Would you say, "Shut the door" to your friend, or would you say,

"Please shut the door?" Become aware of the subtleties of respect (or dis-respect) that are interwoven throughout each interaction with your child. Especially for children with trauma histories who live at a hyper-vigilant level, these little shifts in our responses can be enormous.

Trust that when you are in the moment with your child, not giving a lecture about respect but rather demonstrating respect, you are actually teaching your child and repatterning his neurological response system for the future. This only amplifies the importance of being in the moment! How you treat your child is how you teach your child.

Here are a few great quotes that are pertinent to this discussion:

"Children have never been very good at listening to their elders, but they have never failed to imitate them." – James Baldwin

"Our children cannot be who we tell them to be . . . they can only be who we are." – Joseph Chilton Pearce

"We must become the change we want to see in the world." – Gandhi

Sleep

Q: *Our daughter is two and a half years old. Her early childhood experiences were difficult and she experienced disruption at home. She consistently has difficulty going to sleep at bedtime. She cries and throws tantrums. We sit by her bed until she goes to sleep, but this can take up to two hours and she gets up and down. What makes this difficult is that when she is at daycare, she takes a nap with no problem.*

A: John Bowlby, the father of attachment theory, stated that the first 30 months of a child's life are critical to establishing a secure at-tachment. Trauma at this early age can interrupt and disconnect a child's attachment relationships. Your daughter's experiences have left her in a state of overwhelm and fear at night. For children who have stable and pre-dictable families, home is the "safe base." For your daughter, home may not be this secure base she needs it to be.

This is evident in her being able to sleep away from home, but not at home. Thus, her sleeping patterns are different at home and daycare. It is also important to remember that nighttime is very different from daytime. We process our fears during the night in our dreams. The darkness of night can easily become exaggerated from the light of day.

Your daughter needs more security around sleeping. The most effective security you can offer her is through your relationship with her. The more you can help her to stay connected to you during times of fear and overwhelm, the more you will give her the experiences of learning how to shift from a state of dysregulation to a state of regulation.

Prior to putting her to bed, rock her, soothe her, bottle-feed her. Play soft music. Read a book. Create a consistent routine that you follow every night that offers predictability. Stay present with her and emotionally attuned to her.

Being in her room by herself all night long is too much for her right now. Have her either sleep in your bed with you or move her mattress into your bedroom so she can sleep near you. Find a way to keep her physically closer to you at nighttime.

Have you ever been at home alone at night and found yourself scared? Maybe you heard a noise and your imagination began to go wild, putting you in a state of fear. What if, at that very moment, there was a Rottweiler right next to you, standing guard? Wouldn't you feel safer? Your whole nervous system would settle down. She needs you to be with her in order to protect her and help her settle down, all through the night.

We need to create that kind of security for our children. Past memories, literally ingrained in the cells of their bodies, have created programs for our children that interpret bedtime as a scary event. Rewriting these programs comes through providing measures that are focused on safety, security, and relationship.

Q: *We have the same issues at our house as in the question previous, but my child does not have a significant trauma history, so what about those of us who don't have "major" issues like that?*

A: The basis for a child's sleep issues are fear related. **No matter the circumstance, it takes "listening" to the behavior and recognizing that your child is communicating something to you.**

Below are several examples from parents who have had similar issues. While each story has different details, each parent was able to address the underlying fear, and thus, create peaceful sleep:

"**Linda**" writes: "My son has had a difficult time falling asleep and I've noticed it has been particularly difficult for him during the past several months. We have a nighttime routine that includes cuddling and a back rub, but he still wasn't falling asleep in a reasonable amount of time. Normally, I would stay for 10 or 15 minutes, then assume that he would be falling right to sleep once I left because he is eight years old. One night this past week, he was still awake at 10:30, two and a half hours after he was in bed.

So I decided to go in and talk to him to see if I could help him fall asleep. I was in a fairly regulated state myself and feeling particularly open to him. I went into his room and lay down next to him. There is something about the quiet of night, the darkness and perhaps my own calm state in the space created that really allowed him to open up to me. I asked him what was keeping him awake and what he was afraid of. Within a few minutes, he was crying as many of his fears came pouring out. I stayed in his room for over an hour, but left with him feeling heard and a bit more peaceful than when I first went into his room. I repeated this again the next night. The most amazing thing happened! There was a profound shift in his behavior after the first night and an even bigger shift after the second night! He actually smiled and laughed that next day- something I hadn't seen from him spontaneously in months.

I have continued to go in for an extended time every night this past week. This gives him time to really connect with me and with his fears that he is not as connected to during the day. It has not "fixed" everything, but it has certainly started a new chapter in our journey together. In the past, there has been a great temptation to worry more about what the clock says and feel like I was giving up MY time. But, we've all reaped the benefits during the day of that little extra time at night. I realize now that it is okay for my child to be dependent and that this will truly lead to independence."

"Kim" writes: "We have three children. Our youngest two had sleep problems. I never thought I would do this, but after being kept up half the night when she was about six years old, I finally bought one of those foam rubber couches that turn into a small bed, and let her sleep all night on the bed beside me. Once she was safely beside me, she slept like a LOG within the first few nights, and just as importantly, so did my husband and I! My being next to her was the security she needed. She slept next to me for probably two years, and finally transitioned back into her own bed."

"Diane" writes: "Our son was afraid to sleep in his bed. He presented as the "cool kid," was popular in school and did well there, but was extremely difficult at home. We ended up having him sleep with us in our bedroom and it worked very well. He is now back in his room, although he still gets up once or twice at night and does not sleep very soundly. We are able though, to simply walk him back to his room and tuck him back in. Many people thought we were crazy letting our kids sleep in our room, but they weren't dealing with children who kept them up half the night either!"

"Shirley" writes: "Once we realized that our five-year-old son's bedtime issues were about fear and not about control and defiance, we were able to reduce the stress in our home. Simply acknowledging his fear was all it took. We talked to him about his fears and told him he could come get us if he woke up in the middle of the night. We simply reassured him that we were available to him at anytime of the day or night. He has now gone six nights in a row without sleeping in our bed or waking us up! And this was the child that we struggled with for two years to go sleep in his "big boy bed!" I'm finally able to see that it was my own fear and anxiety of having him sleep with us that was restricting him from being able to shift to his own bed."

Q: *I have a 12 year old with multiple problems including Tourrette's syndrome, severe ADHD, OCD, and possible ODD. She has always had trouble sleeping and until last summer would get up at night and either go through the kitchen looking for sweets or get into trouble in a variety of ways. After listening to your CD's, I realized that this was caused by fear. I started laying down with her at night for a couple of hours and then moving to my own bed. But now she is waking up later and wanting to get in bed with me. Now my sleep is interrupted several times a night and has been for almost six months. I thought she would eventually adjust, but things seem to be worse than ever in terms of her being able to sleep on her own. I did not mention I have been struggling with breast cancer for about a year now and really need my sleep. I would let my husband help, but she does not want him. How do I ease her into a more independent sleeping pattern?*

A: You have done an excellent job of identifying that your daughter's sleep difficulties are related to fear. Many children who wake up in the middle of the night are in a state of dysregulation, hence in a state of fear. They get up, seeking something to soothe them. Just like you or me, what do we eat when we are stressed out? Chocolate? Candy? We go for something sweet.

There is a part of the brain called the nucleus accumbens that programs this quest for sweets. This is the part of the brain where we feel pleasure. There are three tastes that this part of the brain craves: salt, sweets, and fats. Your daughter has been seeking sweets to feel better and relieve the discomfort that comes from being emotionally dysregulated. By lying down with her, you were helping to interrupt this need to regulate through sweets. She was regulating herself through her relationship with you.

Now to address the next issue, she continues to wake up throughout the night and she has not adjusted. Since your daughter has not been able to sleep straight through the night, it is an indication that the core issue has not been addressed. It is not that you have created a child who wants to wake you up in the middle of the night; this shift is simply a part of the process. I would celebrate that she is waking you up instead of going to the sugar in the cabinet.

We then need to look at the next level to ensure that both of you are getting the proper sleep. The question as discussed in Chapter 1 is, "What is driving my child's behavior?"

I believe the core issue is something you mentioned briefly at the very end of your note, "I have been struggling with breast cancer for about a year now." Take the time to understand the impact this statement has on this situation. Since she does not want dad during these times of stress, she is communicating that her fear is with you.

Every child's deepest fear is that of losing a parent. If your daughter has any history of loss or abandonment, this fear is magnified. It is also imperative to be truthful about your own fears. Breast cancer is scary. You are being challenged at a deep emotional and survival level. Opening yourself up to your fear of dying and the other fears that come along with this disease is going to be pivotal in helping your daughter. As you are in touch with your fear, you will then be able to open yourself up to your daughter's fear.

Perhaps her fear is shutting you down and in turn, she is feeling emotionally abandoned. This feeling is unsettling, so she wakes up in the middle of the night. This then stresses you out and adds more stress to her and the negative cycle is in full swing. The cycle of fear is being fed between the two of you and neither of you is getting enough sleep.

Talk to your daughter. Share your fears that have been ignited with the struggle of breast cancer. Create the emotional space for her to tell you what is stirring up inside of her. She may have the words. She may not. As you share your core fears, she'll have the permission to identify her fears and then share them with you. Encourage her to share her emotions with you so that she does not have to keep them all locked up during the day, only to be faced with the fullness of the emotions in the middle of the night.

Stay focused on the core issue instead of the outcome of a more independent sleeping pattern. Sometimes it takes encouraging more dependent behaviors (like connecting at an emotional level) in order to develop independent behaviors.

Feces

Q: *Our five-year-old son has a negative behavior which is rather awkward to discuss, but we desperately need some help and advice. For the past several months, whenever he is supposed to be resting or napping, he "removes" some feces from his body and apparently plays* *with it. The first few occasions, he actually smeared it on the woodwork in his bedroom. Now he seems to "just" smear it in his underwear. We've tried to be non-reactive and non-punitive. We do insist that he clean up his mess, but that doesn't bother him at all. Needless to say, his behavior is rather disgusting. Most importantly, though, is that we simply do not understand why he does this or how to stop it.*

A: Let us "listen" to your son's behavior. It sounds like your son is feeling very scared at naptime and/or bedtime. He has regressed into infantile behavior – "You Stress, You Regress." While this behavior may seem gross, it is actually common in many children with trauma histories to have issues with feces or with urinating. If we understand this behavior as stress induced, we can see that he is doing this in an attempt to regulate. Having him clean up the mess does not address the underlying stress. Ignoring and being non-reactive does not reach the core of the issues, either. Many parents and professionals view negative bodily behaviors such as this as a way of children controlling their parents. It pains me to see this interpretation. He is stressed out and this is only a manifestation of the core fear that engulfs him at naptime.

At the next naptime, perhaps ask him if he gets scared lying there all by himself. Offer to lay with him to begin to soothe his stress and offer regulation simply through your presence. You are a safe place for him and he may need you there to calm his fears and calm his body system. Talk to him softly about how scary it can be to be all alone in bed. It is likely he has some negative experiences and memories linked to naptime or/and bedtime, so this is a great opportunity for healing.

Trust that he will eventually be able to nap by himself...right now he just does not have the sufficient regulatory ability. It is too stressful for him. Be the safe place that he needs you to be and you will see how much he really needs you.

Issues With Eating

Q: *Have you noticed that kids with trauma histories have constant strong cravings for sugar? My daughter has almost an addiction to sweets. Do you have any suggestions for this? I'm not sure whether to appease her cravings by giving her sweets, or to try to remove sweets from her diet (although treats at school are another issue).*

A: Sweet foods are regulatory foods. When in a state of stress, we seek regulation through outside sources, such as food. Ask yourself,

"What do I crave when I'm stressed out and over-whelmed?" Perhaps your "drug of choice" is choco-late or ice cream or cookies. I am certain it is not celery or carrot sticks!

It is important to note that one of the sweetest natural foods is mother's breast milk. The biologi-cally engineered process of breastfeeding an infant is with sweet milk . . . there is a biological connection between sweet food and regulation. It makes perfect sense that a child craving sweets is thus a child crav-ing relationship and attachment.

There is a biological connection between sweet food and regulation.

Additionally, science has shown that stress causes increased cortisol production. Cortisol has been termed the "stress hormone" because it is secreted at higher levels when our stress response system goes into "fight or flight" mode. Children with traumatic histories or those living in stressful environments typically live in this fight or flight survival mode . . . they live in perpetual overdrive.

Since their systems have not been calmed and regulated back into bal-ance, their bodies continue to produce high levels of cortisol. The human body simply is not designed to constantly produce this amount of cortisol, so what happens is that the body will then begin to steal progesterone from the system. This creates a hormonal imbalance and results in a child crav-ing sweets.

In order to find a solution, we need to go back to nature's original design. Just as breastfeeding an infant is so much more than just satisfying a physical need, we can see that appeasing a child's craving for sweets needs to be more than just giving her sweets and hoping for the best.

When your daughter is craving these sweets, recognize this as a time when she is "ripe for relationship." She is craving relationship, attunement, and regulation. She is calling for you, not the sweets. Her behavior is being driven from her need to find safety in connection with you. Address this need by giving her reassurance that she is safe and okay. Let her know that you love her, with-out mentioning the sweets. Work on calming the stress and building your relationship with her. If she absolutely insists on the sweets, sit with her and connect with her while eating the sweets. Have her sit on your lap and feed her as if she is a baby or toddler. You will be transferring her need for sweets through building a relationship with you and helping her regulate through you, not the sweets.

She is calling for you, not the sweets.

You might consider offering her a bottle with something sweet in it, like chocolate milk or juice. It does not matter her age. It is never too late to recreate the parts of her development that she missed. Check in with yourself to acknowledge your fears of this because if you attempt to bottle feed her and you are stressed out, it will not be effective. Once this developmental need is met, children will not need it anymore. You cannot put a jigsaw puzzle together without all the pieces and your daughter cannot move forward in a healthy and regulated manner without all her developmental pieces in place.

You have it in you. Keep listening to the behaviors. They will lead you to the solutions.

Q: *My four-year-old sits down to dinner and says, "I don't like that." He either won't eat at all or won't eat his vegetables. He then gets annoyed, tries to leave the table, whines and refuses to eat. This happens five out of seven nights. How do I respond without consequences?*

A: Meal times are clearly a stressful time for not only your child, but for you as well. Even the thought of dinnertime creates a stress reaction for parents facing this type of situation each night.

Create new experiences around food for you and your child (and your entire family). Have your child sit in your lap to eat. Feed him as you would feed a young toddler. Emotionally your child is probably much younger than four years old. Expecting him to be able to sit down at the table during mealtime is probably well beyond his developmental capabilities.

You might even consider feeding him from a bottle during mealtimes. He may need you to allow him to regress all the way back to infancy in order to create a fresh start. Children with issues around food may have missed some critical experiences that we need to recreate for them. It will give him a stronger foundation from which to grow and reach his full potential.

Recognize that his behavior is being driven from fear and it is not about him rejecting your efforts as a mother to feed him and nurture him. When he says, "I don't like that!" what he is really saying is, "I'm too stressed out to eat this food right now!"

■

More importantly, forcing children to eat during this time or giving consequences around food only creates negative food related issues as adults.

■

We also need to recognize that we should not eat when we are stressed. Our bodies cannot digest the food properly and it becomes toxic in our bodies. More importantly, forcing children to eat during this time or giving consequences around food only creates negative food related issues as adults.

The refusal to eat vegetables has a direct link to being stressed out. As mentioned earlier, we gravitate towards sweets, salts, and fats when we are stressed. Think about this when you are stressed out. What is your regulatory food of choice? Chocolate or broccoli? When we are stressed, we have a difficult time eating vegetables. Think about the last time you were physically sick (where your body was stressed due to illness). Even the thought of eating a salad was enough to make you nauseous.

Try feeding your child outside of mealtimes. Small snacks of carrots and celery during the day can provide nutritious intake for your child. Children are more apt to "graze" than they are to sit and eat an entire meal. While dinnertime is an important time for the entire family to come together, realize that expecting your four-year-old to be engaged at this point in his development is only creating a negative experience for everyone.

As you gain a deeper understanding of the stress driving your child's behavior, you will find more solutions that work for your family. Stay focused on your child's needs and "listen" to his behavior and there you will find the answers.

Keep focused on calming your child's environment around mealtime. This will in turn help your son settle his nervous system which will naturally bring back his appetite and desire to eat.

Q: *I am the single mother of a four-year-old daughter. The one thing that drives me crazy about my daughter is her constant craving for sweets. I realize this could be a normal four-year-old thing. She does not horde candy or other food, but she is constantly asking for chocolate and other sweet things. Given the opportunity I believe she would eat nothing but sweets, and in fact, she will refuse meals and then later ask for chocolate. As a parent I am not sure how to handle this behavior. Is it best to not allow any chocolate or candy/cookies in our home? Should I limit the amount she is allowed to have in a 24-hour period? Should I allow her to have sweets only after she has eaten healthy food? Or should I just look at this as a need she has to be nurtured by me and let her have the chocolate? I am quite overweight myself and have been since I was a child. I know that is where some of my distress over this issue comes from.*

A: Your daughter's craving for sweets is a communication of her need to strengthen her relationship with you. Unfortunately, the more she communicates in this way, the more stressed out you become. The more stressed out you become, the more she craves sweets. The negative neurological feedback loop is then in full swing and spiraling down fast.

The last sentence in your question is the key to interrupting this negative loop and you are absolutely on the right track in recognizing the fear you bring to this situation. It is hard to look beyond the chocolate when you fear your child becoming overweight. You have struggled with your weight since childhood and I am certain suffered social ridiculing as a result of this. Although it is out of a loving intent to not have your child experience the same, the truth is that your fear and negative thoughts of this happening are actually increasing the chances of this becoming a reality for your daughter.

As you are able to set your own fear aside, you will see the situation with more clarity. It is often our past fear from a particular experience that creates the same exact situation with our children.

Your daughter is giving you the chance to also address your own weight issues. You may not consciously be asking for this "opportunity," yet it is typically the case that children present with identical issues as their parents. That is the gift our children bring to us.

To work through this situation with your daughter, I would suggest having your daughter sit on your lap while you feed her something sweet. You can try something like apples or strawberries that are naturally sweet, but if she insists on chocolate, then chocolate it is. The idea is to transfer her being satisfied by sweets to her being satisfied by her connection with you. As you nurture her through this interaction, she will learn to calm her system through her relationship with you, not through the chocolate. Her continual desire to have chocolate is similar to the alcoholic desperately needing his next drink in order to be okay.

When you say, "this is our last piece" and she still reacts as if she is going to die without more chocolate, work to soothe her stress instead of rationalizing with her. Your response may be, "The chocolate does taste so good and I know it helps you to calm down. May I give you a hug so you know you're going to be okay?" **Acknowledge the boundary you have established, give her permission to be upset, validate her reaction, and love her through it.**

Regressive Behaviors

Q: *I understand the concept that children may sometimes revisit a prior developmental stage when dealing with stress. You have said to be present with them. How do you do that? For example, if an eight-year-old boy is acting like a four-year-old, how can a parent demonstrate to the child that the parent is with him?*

A: To be present with a child is simply to be there listening, connecting, and loving. This state of love requires us to be free from judgment, free from "fixing" the child or making him different, and free from giving direction on how to act differently. Think about a time you called your best friend when you were upset. You did not want to hear any solutions; you did not want to hear how you could have acted differently. All you needed her to do was simply listen to you, validate you, and ask you how bad you really felt. This is what your son needs from you when he is regressing and in a stress response mode. Sit with him, tell him you are just there to be with him, and allow him his emotional space to find his own way back to being an eight-year-old. Instead of being the parent that rationalizes, minimizes, or normalizes his situation, be the parent who validates, affirms, and authenticates his experience. (see *Beyond Consequences, Logic, and Control, Volume 2,* Chapter 3, "Staying in the Present Moment")

Q: *My adopted son (six-years-old) urinates in the hall, dining room, etc. I never observe him doing it but I find the "evidence" later. What can I do?*

A: Two immediate thoughts come to mind with your son. First, the bathroom is a notorious place for abuse to occur, leaving children terrified of going into the bathroom. Second, inappropriate urinating is a profoundly regressive behavior.

The first issue to address is to create safety for your son in the bathroom. Acknowledge his fear and validate it, "Son, it seems like going into the bathroom can be *really* scary. I want to make sure you're safe while you're in there and not alone in your fear." Offer to go into the bathroom with him. If you are his mother and he expresses the need for privacy, stay right outside the door while he is in there. Leave the door cracked so he can hear you. Talk to him softly, assuring him all the while, so he knows where you are.

If you have punished him or reacted in anger in the past for his urinating, apologize to him and let him know you should have done more to help him feel safe. The goal is to make yourself a safe place for him to come to when he needs to go to the bathroom. Ask him to come get you when he needs to go to the restroom so you can make it safe for him. Make a commitment to be mindful of the time and regularly ask him if he might need to use the restroom.

Many times children with trauma histories, especially those who experienced neglect and sexual abuse, lose contact with their bodily functions. In the past, they escaped the pain by disconnecting from their physical bodies. It takes helping them reconnect to their body's natural rhythms.

These natural bodily rhythms are known as circadian rhythms-the body's biological cycling of waking and sleeping, eating and drinking, maintaining body temperature, controlling urination, etc. during a 24-hour period. Stress can interrupt this cycle, so the more that can be done to create an environment that reduces the stress, the body will have more opportunity to shift back into sync with its natural rhythms.

Children coming out of orphanages are often out of sync with their daily rhythms. Their circadian rhythms were reprogrammed by the regimented structure of institutionalized life. They too need the opportunity to become more aligned with their organic bodily functions.

The second point is that your son's development has been arrested. His trauma has prevented him from truly being at a six-year-old level. In order to help him move forward in his growth process, his foundation needs to be secured through a secure relationship with you.

Going back and revisiting early developmental activities is imperative for his system to learn to regulate. He is not equipped to regulate his body like other six-year-olds who have been in loving, nurturing, and predictable environments. It is important to understand this because when you expect him to be a six-year-old, you will become frustrated and easily angered at his infantile behaviors.

I encourage you to offer him nurturing activities that you would typically do for a one-year-old. Hold him, rock him, bottle feed him, sing to him, cuddle with him. These are regulatory activities. As you help him regulate, his nervous system will return to a state of calm instead of a state of heightened arousal. He cannot do it on his own. He needs a parent to do this for him, just as any one-year-old would need it.

As your son has more positive experiences with you and his body is given assistance in regulating its natural functions, these urinating behaviors will disappear. Remember that due to his early life experiences, he actually has no other choice than to do what he is doing. Accepting where he is in this moment will create peace in your home and jumpstart you both to a better relationship, giving his body the opportunity to reconnect and realign naturally.

The Need for Certainty

Q: *What do you do with a child who is so compelled to a repetitious behavior that he can't be redirected to the task at hand?*

A: As humans, one of our basic primal needs is that of certainty. It feels good to know for certain what is going to happen, when it is going to happen, and how it is going to happen. We also seek certainty through our behaviors and actions. For some, repetitive behaviors create certainty which reduces the level of internal fear. OCD (obsessive compulsive disorder) is about an intense need for certainty. For others, food creates certainty. Food makes us feel good, thus gives us a feeling of certainty. Additionally, many parents seek certainty through controlling parenting techniques.

On the other hand, uncertainty is a basic human need as well but only if there is enough certainty in our lives to create a balance between the two. For most of us, we enjoy an occasional surprise; it creates excitement. We like change, to a small degree, because it creates variety in our lives. For some, a higher level of uncertainty creates a rush of being "alive" like riding a roller coaster, watching a scary movie, or even jumping out of an airplane.

For children with earlier experiences of unpredictability, chaos, and disruption in their lives, they have experienced an over abundance of uncertainty. There has not been a balance between the amount of uncertainty and certainty in their lives. If an imbalance of the two creates a level of fear for the average adult then it is understandable for a child, with limited coping skills, such an imbalance creates an exponential amount of fear.

The result is a child who will constantly seek certainty, at all costs. He is working to live in a heightened state of certainty in order to calm the fear of uncertainty that is programmed in his nervous system.

When we as parents try to redirect this behavior, we are creating yet more uncertainty. The child, in his desperate attempt to return to a state of balance and regulation, will resist the parent and refuse to be redirected. The parent typically interprets this as "bad" behavior, "defiant" behavior, or "disrespectful" behavior. Worse, the parent takes this lack of responsiveness personally as if the child is behaving in this manner simply to push the parent's buttons or to be revengeful.

The negative neurological feedback loop is thus in full swing. Both the parent and the child are working to attain certainty, yet they are both doing it from a self-absorbed framework. The relationship becomes more strained, thus breeding more uncertainty.

If the parent can understand that the child is simply working to create certainty in his uncertain world, this negative loop can be interrupted. The parent can acknowledge that the compelling behavior (as given in this question) is helping the child feel better and that switching to a new task is incredibly difficult and scary. A conversation might look like this:

Mom: "Tommy, it is going to be time for us to go out and rake leaves in a few minutes."

Tommy: *Ignores his mom and continues to keep pushing his Hot Wheels up and down the hallway, over and over again.*

Mom: *Sitting down near Tommy, acknowledging his behavior,* "You like running your cars up and down this hallway, don't you? I think you've been doing it for over an hour. Wow! That does look like fun and I bet it makes you feel good."

Tommy: "I don't want to go rake leaves."

Mom: "I know. It isn't easy changing from one activity that makes you feel good to another activity that you don't even like."

Tommy: "I hate raking leaves."

Mom: "I know. I want to help you today. I don't want you to feel so overwhelmed with this type of stuff anymore. If I'm with you, I'm certain it will be easier for you."

Tommy: "Humph"

Mom: "How about we do this in about five minutes?"

Mom works to connect with Tommy's fears and acknowledges his struggle in shifting to a different activity. She creates certainty by being with him now while promising to be with him during the new activity. Through their relationship, she is working to create the certainty he is seeking through the toy cars. Her goal is to help Tommy shift from using the toys as security to using her relationship with him as the security. Giving him five minutes also gives Tommy emotional space to consider making this change and time to process this change, which reduces the element of surprise.

As human beings, we are constantly working to create balance in our lives. Your children's behaviors are often times reflective of this need for balance. Look beyond the typical interpretations of defiance, disrespect, and retaliation, to identify the significance of your child's behaviors. When you can do this, you put yourself in the most powerful position – the position of a committed, loving, and understanding parent.

Hygiene

Q: *My 14-year-old daughter was adopted at eight months from Russia. She suffered severe neglect and was still in the hospital at that time and weighed nine pounds. At 12 years old, she started her menstrual cycle but has not been able to manage her self-care in this area in terms of using pads or any other related hygiene products. We are at the point where I have to have her show me that she has a pad on but I have to periodically check because she will go in another room and take it off. Consequently, she soils undergarments, clothing, and places where she sits. Do you have any suggestions or ideas for a way to approach this?*

A: Your daughter has quite a traumatic history. Nine pounds at eight months old is a child who was scheduled to die. I mention this because we cannot ever minimize the impact this is having on her development. She is emotionally too immature to be able to handle her menstrual cycle and many times children resist growing up because they inherently know they need to capture pieces of their childhood before moving forward.

First, connect with her about not wanting to grow up. I would suggest rocking her and holding her. She may need to regress in order to be able to move forward in her development. Talk to her about how you missed being able to care for her when she was a baby. Apologize for not being able to be there and let your heart sink into how you would have done anything to prevent this from happening to her. Tell her you want to do everything now to make sure she gets what she missed with you. If you are married, have your spouse do the same. Rock her and reconnect with her. You all have been stressed with this menstrual cycle issue. The resistance to growing up can also be a fear of having to be responsible as an adult. This can be so overwhelming for children. Let her know that she can stay with you for as long as she needs to. If she has the idea that at 18 she is on her own (that is only four years away), this may be triggering the resistance. Tell her she can live with you forever (yes, this may bring up your own fears, but she will not really need to do this).

Second, avoid the issue of changing her pad from a cognitive framework. Just do it for her right now. Getting her to show you is too threatening and controlling for what she can handle. Your approach would be similar to changing a baby's diaper. You can say, "I realize this whole changing your pad thing is way too much, sweetheart. How about I just do it for you. Let me handle it." Take responsibility for her and when the stress is removed, she'll soon be able to do it on her own. This takes a big commitment on your part to keep up with it. Just remember that it is like asking a baby to change her own diaper. Impossible.

I would suspect that this issue with her menstrual cycle is not isolated and that she becomes easily overwhelmed in all parts of her life. The more you can do to reduce the amount of stress in all areas of her life, the more she will have the space to mature and develop. **Trust that by reducing her load of responsibility and helping her at this point, she will progress and develop a greater capacity within herself to be able to handle these types of issues on her own in the future.** We all have to learn how to crawl before we can walk and for some of us, especially your daughter, it will be a slower path due to an intense history of trauma.

Runaways

Q: *I have a 15-year-old son who has established a pattern of running away. I've been advised by his therapist to call the police when this occurs. What do you suggest?*

A: Running away is indicative of a child who has entered a fear state. When we, and all animals in the animal kingdom become threatened, we go into a primitive response called the "Fight or Flight" response. It is an inborn genetic response which helps us to protect ourselves throughout our lives. It is a survival response.

Your therapist is recommending a technique that is from the traditional view. Calling the police will only create more dysregulation, less safety, and feed more fear into an already fearful child. Rather, help him to see how threatened he feels at the moment before he takes off. Acknowledge that he feels that this is his only solution but you want to be able to help him through it this time.

When this is understood, it is clear that calling the police on a child in this survival response pattern should never be recommended. How would calling the police be helpful to a child who is simply acting from his body's primitive, automatic, inborn response? Your child is acting from an unconscious level. It is not a conscious response; it is a unconscious reaction. Addressing it from an authoritative and fear-based approach will only keep your child in this pattern; hence, you described it as an "established pattern."

We have somehow come to believe that we can force change by provoking fear and threat. This is completely unnatural. Have you ever seen nature force a seedling to grow? You simply cannot force a child (or an adult) into compliance. This is a choice that has to come from an internal place from within that person.

To give such advice about sending the police is an example of doing the same thing over and over again, while expecting a different result (this of course, is the definition of insanity). According to a recent Washington Post report, more than one in 100 adults in the United States are now in jail or prison. This is an all time high. When are we going to realize that this is not working?

Our own fear keeps us in a constricted place, locked in from seeing other alternatives. Fear keeps us in a loop of trying harder, "upping the ante," and driving more consequences in order to get our children to behave and to be compliant. As young children, it started by picking them up and putting them in the time-out chair. When they got too old to sit in time out, we began removing privileges in order to get them to comply. When this became ineffective with a "whatever" response from them, we then increased the stakes and grounded them for a week. Finally, as teenagers, they realized they had the ability to just leave and run away. Now we take massive fear-driven action and call the police.

Love has not been a part of the solution . . . that is why the cycle has continued. If you want to end the cyclical turmoil in a family, put love into action. Unfortunately, many of us have no blueprint for what this looks like, so it challenges us at a deep level to consider that it would actually work.

The next time your son runs away (and I also suggest looking closely at the circumstances that led up to this event and determine how to reduce the fear contributing to the situation), I want you to plan a celebration for his return. Instead of calling the police, call the caterer! Seriously, bake a cake or some cookies. Go to the party store and buy some balloons. Make a banner that says, "Welcome home, son. We missed you."

When a child returns, what we typically do is dump our fear onto the child. Instead of saying, "I was scared for you," we say, "How dare you leave this house and not tell us where you were going!" We need to realize that it took a tremendous amount of courage for the child to walk back into that door, knowing the parent was going to lecture him about everything he had done wrong.

> *Know that when he feels heard, he will be able to hear you.*

Put love into action when he walks in the next time. "Son, I'm so glad you're home. We missed you." It takes putting your fear aside and getting down to your core feelings. You *did* miss him. You *are* glad he is home. Let him know how special he is in your life. If you have lost these loving feelings towards your child due to the intense dysregulation going on, revisit pictures of when he was younger and when times were calmer and more pleasant. Get yourself back into a loving place with him.

Later in the day, take the time to be with your child and listen to him. Talk about what it is that drives him to leave. Really listen to him. Give him space to voice himself. Stay out of being defensive. Know that when he feels heard, he will be able to hear you. When you give him the gift of being understood, you can then take the opportunity to express your fear. "I just get so scared when you leave. When I don't know where you are, I feel so powerless and I can't do anything to help you at that point."

Be courageous enough to try something different. You have the capacity to interrupt the negative loop and change this established pattern with your child. It takes trusting that love never fails.

Victimhood and Blame

Q: *As a therapist, I work with a family with two children. The older child is well regulated and compliant. The second child has a traumatic birth experience and has challenging behaviors. The parents want to discipline the second child exactly the same way they do their well-attached, well-behaved older child, because it's "not fair" otherwise. I have talked about how and why time-outs are injurious for their younger child, why severe consequences such as writing an extreme number of sentences is not a fair punishment for a child who has trauma-related learning disabilities, but I just don't seem to get through. Any suggestions?*

■

Any child is seeking regulation when acting out negatively.

■

A: Have they considered switching their parenting paradigm for their first child? Just because the old traditional style of parenting that focuses on changing the child's behaviors works for some children, does not mean that it works to build strong relationships. Any child is seeking regulation when acting out negatively.

Negative behavior is a communication of something much deeper than just "being ugly" or "being defiant." I advocate "time-in" for all children. In fact, I advocate time-in for adults; I advocate time-in for myself when I'm feeling dysregulated. It takes a commitment to listening rather than correcting.

For example, if I'm hungry, I listen to my body and I respond to this communication by eating and satisfying my hunger. Would it make sense for me to react to hunger pains by fasting for the next 12 hours as a punishment for having hunger pains? Absolutely not. Yet, this is what traditional parenting teaches us to do with our children. When our children act in ways that make us feel uncomfortable (just as hunger pains are uncomfortable), instead of responding in a way to address this communication, we remove privileges or put them in time-out (like having ourselves fast because of the hunger pains). Responsive and love-based parenting recognizes that negative communication is a request for love, validation, reassurance, safety, help, or more simply, a request for regulation.

Children are not misbehaving from a conscious place, but from an unconscious place of seeking regulation. The family in this question has an opportunity to build stronger relationships with their first child now that their second child has shown them how detrimental traditional parenting can be. Perhaps if they look through the lens of seeing this second child as a gift to help build their family, instead of feeling like victims to this child, the entire family system will be happier and more regulated.

When stress overflows in a home, a mentality of "victimhood" often becomes the dominant paradigm. In such a shift, there is typically one child who becomes the target. We need to realize that we are only victims if we choose to be victims. **It is our personal responsibility as parents to recognize that nothing is happenstance. What is, is.** We must recognize our own fears and our own shortcomings instead of shifting this blame onto our child.

Many parents come into adulthood with childhood patterns of blame and victimhood. These patterns and beliefs then go into autopilot when we become stressed and overwhelmed. Peace, healing, and strong relationships begin with our own self-healing, our own self-validation, and our own self-love. We cannot expect our children to be our source of love, validation, and feelings of "being all right."

In this example, the older child was able to feed the parents with all of this, making the parents feel good. Yet the younger child was not able to feed the parents with this relational nutrition. What is hap-pening is that the second child is now viewed as the source of this "malnutrition" and is getting blamed for the parents lack of own self-understanding, self-

We cannot give what we have not received.

love, self-validation, and self-acceptance. The reality is that the only person who can reject us is ourselves and conversely, the first place for us to find unconditional and consistent love is within ourselves.

For this family, remember that resistance is only fear. Help them to see that this second child has a stress response system that has been compro-mised due to his early experiences. Help them to relate to their own feelings of inadequacy and their own perceptions of feeling like failures. Help them to see that their second child is in great need of support, love, and understanding.

The bottom line is this: We cannot give what we have not received. Thus this second child needs more reassurance and love to calm his nervous system. He does not have the same regulatory capacity as his older brother. His disruptive behaviors have created a dynamic where he feels second best and rejected. He does not feel loved unconditionally, thus, he cannot give what he has not yet received.

Love, free of blame, free of conditions, and free of expecta-tions, is always the answer to healing.

Q: *It has been so difficult to get our 24-year-old daughter to "receive" our love. It is available but she often twists what we say around and attributes some mean motive to it or makes it into something totally different than intended. Do you have any suggestions?*

A: I would suggest that life is presenting you with a chance to practice and truly understand unconditional love. It is about loving someone without expecting anything in return and being confident that your loving message will not fail, even when the immediate response shows no sign of change. Our biggest calling is to love extravagantly with hope and certainty. Her rejection of your love is not about rejecting you. She is rejecting herself.

■

The more you become a safe place for her, the less she will have reason to twist your intentions.

■

Your responsibility is to simply love her, with no undertones of rejection, anger, or fear in return. Love has to be sincere. As you continue to love her with patience and kindness, expecting nothing in return, you are making yourself safe for her. The more you become a safe place for her, the less she will have reason to twist your intentions. You are working to re-pattern her ability to receive love. I realize it is hard and you worry for her future, but the more you are able to stay in the present, accepting her simply because she is your child, the more trust you are creating for positive change in the future. Healing is not just a journey, it is a workshop. So "work" to stay in a place of love, forgiveness, and faith, and she will find her way.

Q: *How do you deal with a victim mentality in a teenager?*

A: We live in a blame oriented/victimized society. It is our culture to look at others as if they are the ones preventing us from being happy and they are the ones blocking us from being successful. For such an individualistic society, it is an interesting dichotomy to also be entrenched in a society where individuals refuse to take personal responsibility.

Additionally, simply by the nature of being a teen, this victimhood stance is developmentally appropriate. Teens today have a stronger sense of entitlement than teens in the past. They expect their parents to take care of them and they have an understanding that parents are not allowed to hurt them. They also expect their parents to protect them. When these expectations are not met, the result is to shift into a heightened sense of victimhood.

When we stop to consider these factors, it is perfectly natural for teens who have not fully connected with their families or had their needs met to feel like victims. Helping a teenager move out of this framework will require parents to first shift out of feeling like victims to their teen. The sense of victimhood is often present on both sides of the parent/child dyad.

Teenagers (and children) need their parents to take responsibility for them. Many teens have never had a parent truly take responsibility for the events of the past (painful medical procedures, divorce, loss of another parent, abuse, etc). While many of these events are simply, "life," this does not minimize that these experiences were painful, unpredictable, and scary for the teen. If someone hits you with a baseball bat by accident, rather than on purpose, you do not feel less pain. From the teen's perspective, he needs the parent to take responsibility in order to move forward in relationship. That is the job of the parent.

The teen needs the parent to say, "I'm sorry I wasn't able to make it easier for you. I'm so sorry this happened to you."

Memories of negative experiences are stored in a fragmented and disorganized way, so the linear timeline of events has no bearing. All the teen knows is that she was hurt and the parents who are asking him to trust them and love them did not stop the pain or have not been able to make it better for him.

To truly understand this perspective, it requires the parent to release the concept of blame. Thoughts of, *"There was nothing I could have done about it."* or *"It wasn't my fault."* negate the fact that the child's healing process requires someone taking responsibility. The teen just needs the parent to make an apology.

Offer to listen to your teen's victim mentality. Work to understand what the core issue is behind this attitude. It is likely that what your teen is saying at a subconscious level is: *"I need someone to take care of me and I'm the way I am because I wasn't loved unconditionally. I have felt unworthy and unlovable. You're expecting me to grow up and I can't do that yet. More importantly, I'm scared I won't be better before I turn 18 and that is only a few years away."*

Reach out to your teen at his emotional age. Take responsibility for him and meet him in his victimhood instead of lecturing him as to why he has no right to have such an attitude. Connect with him in relationship through understanding, patience, acceptance, spending time together, and tolerance. Meeting his needs will give him the security to shift out of this victimhood place and secure his foundation in order to be a responsible and giving adult.

Animal Killing

Q: *I adopted a sibling group of four who were severely abused and neglected. My nine year old is very aggressive and doesn't feel safe unless he has some kind of a weapon. I keep reminding him this is a safe place. He steals things to hurt people (pocket knives), even things that have no meaning. This is so scary and I didn't want to believe it. But then our family cat disappeared. My son actually helped all of us search for the cat, put up posters, and everything. Days later he was laughing and told us he killed the cat and it is not ever coming back. How do I handle this? How do I get him to feel safe so he doesn't need to hurt people that care about him? I do love him even after all he has put this family through. I just don't know how to help him with this.*

A: Fear is an acronym for "False Evidence Appearing Real" (FEAR). This fits exactly for your son's situation. I realize pocket knives and a dead cat are real on the surface and quite scary when in the midst of it. However, in order to help your son, we have to look at the core issues driving his behavior. **If all we can see is the external evidence that puts us into a state of fear, we will not be able to see the internal reality of the fear within our children.**

I believe we have a wise instinctual part in each one of us and when you say "I didn't want to believe it," then don't. Stop fighting yourself. Your inner wisdom is telling you that it is just an illusion. **Your son is not out to kill; he is out to protect.** He is literally terrified.

What would it be like if you lived your life feeling like everyone around you was going to hurt you or kill you? His blueprint says that family members are unsafe. You are his family, therefore, you are unsafe. He lives in a black and white world due to his early history of neglect. The mind is like a computer and it runs off the programs installed from our early experiences. He does not know any different.

■

It takes revealing the FEAR in order to return to love and security.

■

Have you ever had thoughts running through your mind, depicting a scenario of you trapped inside your home with an intruder, unable to get help? You probably pictured yourself doing something to protect yourself, no matter how terrible – possibly going to the kitchen to grab a butcher knife. Not easy thoughts, but this is how we think when we are creating our survival plan.

You mentioned that you keep reminding him "this is a safe place." This is your reality, not his, and the more you try to convince him of it, the more resistant he will become. I encourage you to allow him the space, both verbally and emotionally, to let him tell you how unsafe he feels. *"Son, objects like this (pointing to the knife he has in hand) help you feel safe, don't they? I'm starting to understand how scared you really are. You feel like you need to protect yourself. You probably feel like someone is going to kill you. Tell me how bad that is for you. You're not in trouble. You're not going anywhere. I just need to know how bad it is for you."* Be as direct as you can because this is his language. Connect with the depth of his fear.

Opening the conversation to allow for this direct talk will help him work to shift his interpretation of his new life with you. It takes revealing the FEAR in order to return to love and security. Blocked feelings will inhibit change.

Children kill animals when they feel like the animal is going to kill them. This is not unusual for children who suffer severe trauma. Perhaps your son was playing with the cat and became overwhelmed, getting too rough with the cat, and the cat scratched him or gave him a warning. BAM! His window of stress tolerance is so small that immediately that cat became the mountain lion ready to eat and kill him (remember that stress causes confused and distorted thinking). His only line of defense was to kill the cat first.

Children like your son need to have supervision around animals in order to keep both the animal and the child safe. I would apologize to your son, letting him know that you did not help to keep him safe while he was with the family cat. Express that it must have been a horrifying experience for him and that you had no idea that he felt like the cat was going to kill him or that he has such a need to be powerful. Take responsibility for not being able to protect him and let him know he is okay.

Once his stress response system calmed down, he realized the magnitude of what he had done. Not having a secure relationship with you, once again he had no where to go with this outpouring of fear. Helping out with the posters and acting as if he had no idea what happened to the cat was him trying to mask the fear and make it all better. He might have been thinking, "If I help out, then everything will be alright." Children lie and cover up in order to keep from getting consequences, or in many adopted children's cases, to keep from getting sent away again.

But then the level of fear continued to rise and became too great. The emotional intensity was far too much so he went to laughter instead. One way children (and adults) resort to releasing uncomfortable emotional energy is by laughing. Hence, your son could not contain the fear anymore and laughed about the cat. Have you ever laughed when you were nervous or had friends give a distorted laugh about a serious issue? This is exactly the same as what happened with your son.

Your son was trapped in a negative neurological feedback loop. Each lie built more negativity and each act of defiance bred more fear. He was swinging from one end of the emotional continuum to the other, completely dysregulated and trapped. His behaviors are telling you that he does not have the ability to stop this train. He needs your help.

Yet, if you are afraid of him, he will perceive you as a threat. When you lift the veil of illusion by shifting your interpretation of this situation and connect with his terror, then you will have all the power to help him. Breathe deeply and allow yourself to release the interpretation that he wants to kill you or someone in your family. Breathe deeply again and say, "My son is fighting for his life. He is terrified." Feel your body shift from fear to love. Take this new, "safer you," into your son's space. See his fear. Feel his fear. Connect with his fear, both verbally and mentally.

Your words, "after all he has put this family through," show that your level of stress has shifted you into a place of victimhood. The original victim was your son who was abused and neglected early in his life when he should have been nurtured and loved. He is only being who he has been taught to be and as you respond to him from a place of love and truth, you will both be victors instead of victims.

Sibling Rivalry

Q: *How should we respond to my seven-year-old daughter when she "roars" or "hisses" or "growls" at our three-year-old son? She will put her fist in her brother's face when she roars at him. She will poke him in the arm but never enough to physically hurt him.*

A: Your daughter's behavior is indicative of her being scared (thus, she gives a threatening animal sound and uses her physical body to threaten her brother). I encourage you not to address the actual behavior, but address her fear. Pull her closer to you, hold her, hug her, and tell her you love her and that she is going to be okay. Later that day, when she is calm and regulated, ask her what made her upset and help her talk about the feelings she is having, giving her more socially appropriate ways to handle her fears.

Sibling rivalry comes down to children feeling threatened, especially children with trauma backgrounds where emotional needs and physical needs were rarely met in their previous experiences. Work to see your children as feeling as if they have to be "king" or "queen" of the pack simply because if they do not, they will die. It really is this intense for them. It is not about the behavior, so address the core issue of safety and security. Spend 10 minutes in the morning with your child, 20 minutes after school or work, and then 10 minutes at bedtime. This is at least 40 minutes each day with each of your children, simply connecting and being in their worlds. This is a very effective tool in helping children calm their fear about their safety in the family. During this time with each child, work to be present with that child. Let your child take the lead in the conversation; let your child have this time all to himself in order to feel special and important to you.

Cell Phones

Q: *Recently, we gave our 14-year-old son a cell phone. He is so sharp that he figured out how to get onto the Internet through his phone. I didn't even know you could get on the Internet. I just thought it was a phone. Without knowing, he ran up a $2,500 bill. What should we do now?*

A: We have to step back from the financial piece and center ourselves on what is more important here. Is your relationship with your son worth more than $2,500? The reason I ask this is because when we look at a response to this situation, we have to stay focused on developing a trusting and strong relationship between you and your son.

First, reacting back at your son through punitive fear-based parenting techniques puts all the blame on your child. Part of parenting is being responsible and creating safe environments for our children. As you mentioned, the phone you gave him had Internet access. I realize you did not know this; however, the access was still there for him. I would suggest sitting down with him and first apologizing that you gave him a phone that had the ability to gain access to the Internet and that you should have blocked the access prior to giving it to him.

Second, I am certain your son had no idea he was charging up such a huge bill. We have to remember that children want to please their parents more than anyone else on this planet and when things go "amuck," it is not because of malicious intent. Children are curious and resourceful. This is a trait we do not want to squash, but preserve and help to contain within appropriate boundaries, especially within financial boundaries.

Third, we need to look at why your son was on the Internet for such long periods of time. We are social beings and we have a biological need to connect in relationship. When the relationships around us are limited, weak, or lack joy, we will seek them through other means. It is also developmentally appropriate for teenagers to seek social interaction and to seek it in abundance. This is a communication to you as a parent that efforts need to be made to firm up this relationship in order to build trust, connection, and "fun" between you and him.

Implementing consequences for this extraordinary bill would only drive a wedge between you and your child. Peaceful conversations are needed where you take responsibility for your part in this weak relationship. It might sound like this: "Son, spending this amount of time on the Internet only tells me I'm not doing a good job of connecting with you right here in our own home. I want to spend more time with you, do more with you, and help you learn how to trust me more. I'm sorry for not realizing this sooner."

You are asking, "What about teaching my son responsibility for his actions?" Remember that in order for children to learn responsibility, it takes a parent first being responsible for him. In doing the aforementioned items, you are teaching an enormous lesson about responsibility.

Another lesson is to teach your son how to think through situations with better judgment. Talk to him about how you need him to come to you when he discovers new things, like getting on the Internet. There will be more situations in these next several years where he will be faced with something novel. For example, if he found a bag of drugs, would you want him to feel safe enough to come to you with it instead of trying some of it on his own? Work on building his trust of you and assuring him of your willingness to help him through new and unfamiliar situations, no matter how difficult it may seem at the time. It is imperative that he knows he will NOT get into trouble by coming to you. "Son, I want to be here to help you through everything. I want to be a safe place for you to come to when you are facing decisions. When you don't come to me, I feel sad because then I cannot help you. I want to help you as a parent. I want to be here for you."

This would actually be a great opportunity to build and strengthen your relationship by working together to pay the $2,500 bill. Sit down with your son and explain that you both had a part in this and that you will both work together to pay it off. You might help him start his own lawn care service or sell stuff around the house on eBay (with your assistance). We sometimes miss these parent/child bonding opportunities because we are so outraged, placing 100% of the blame on our child.

We must recognize that life presents us with situations everyday in order to deepen our relationships with our children.

If you decide to take the phone away to prevent any further charges, the way in which you implement this decision is critical. Instead of saying, "You're not responsible enough to have a phone, we are taking it away from you," (blaming, judgmental, controlling, and harsh) you might consider saying it in a more responsive way, "Having this phone is quite overwhelming right now. To make sure you're safe and we're all okay, we are not going to have this extra phone for awhile." Setting boundaries through love is what our children need. What they do not need is for us to set boundaries through blame, control, and fear.

Only you can be the one who makes this experience a positive one with your child. Parenting at a higher level of consciousness takes first loving ourselves so deeply that when our children do the things they do, we do not have to react. We do not have to interpret the behavior as rejection. We do not have to see ourselves as a "bad or ineffective" parent. We love ourselves so much that we are unshakable and we are able to respond from a place of unconditional love, taking responsibility through understanding, acceptance, patience, kindness, and flexibility.

We must recognize that life presents us with situations everyday in order to deepen our relationships with our children. When we miss these opportunities, the situations will only present themselves again, but each time they come back, they will become more difficult until we finally get the point and embrace the opportunity to build our relationship with our child. Your relationship with your child is vital and absolutely the key to his mental, emotional, physical, and spiritual development. It is all within you to create this for your child.

Chores

Q: *Are chores the most appropriate way to deal with issues when you have tried everything else and some sort of consequences are needed for things like not following directions and being disrespectful, etc?*

A: This is a great question and one that is asked often. When we feel like the implementation of the *Beyond Consequences* model is not working, we easily shift back to our old parenting paradigm of giving consequences. This is because when we stress, we regress.

When it is not "working," this is probably the worst time to go back to using consequences-- because if it is not working, then you are most likely more stressed out than ever. Implementing a consequence when you are stressed out only ensures a disconnect in your relationship with your child.

When we truly understand the paradigm of love and fear and understand that children act out negatively from an unconscious place, then the mere thought of a consequence makes no sense. If children do not consciously misbehave then how can we consequent them? It is like consequencing your child for having the hiccups. That would be absurd!

Children act out to receive love, attention, acceptance, security, and validation. When you give consequences in order to control a child's behavior, you are actually satisfying their need for attention, just in a negative way. **Consider**

that any form of concentrated attention is interpreted as love. Do you want their concentrated attention to be love or fear (positive or negative)?

When you feel yourself shifting back and wanting to end it all by giving one big fat consequence, just stop and slow down. Take three deep breaths. Acknowledge your state of complete frustration. Acknowledge that you feel ineffective as a parent and out of control. When we shift into a fear state, we seek to gain control through fear-based techniques. Yet, the reality is that true control comes through loving influence, not through controlling directives.

The next step is to ask yourself, "What am I afraid of?" or "What is the real issue here?" Process through your fears, openly, honestly, and without judgment. Once you can see your own fear, you will return to being able to see your child's fear.

When you shift back into this state of love, which offers peace for yourself, you will realign your understanding that your child is working from fear, not conscious awareness.

As you are able to calm yourself and interact with your child by adding positive energy, you will be 100% more effective. As your child calms down and returns to a state of love, you then have your opportunity to teach the lesson. That is the time to talk about how the negative behavior and disrespectful talk are inappropriate.

Your child wants to please you more than anyone else on this planet. It is just hard, if not impossible, to believe this when they are irate and disrespectful. Yet, it is our responsibility as parents to provide the environment to allow this to come to the surface. With a sensitive child, the challenge of creating such an environment is simply magnified at an exponential level. Yet, that is the power of unconditional love – to overcome all levels of fear.

School Issues

Q: *Which educational avenue do you recommend: home education, public school, or private school? Our counselor/therapist recommended a school setting to reduce conflict (we have been home schooling).*

A: Each child's educational plan should be individualized according to the child's needs. On this basis, it is impossible to recommend one educational avenue over another. Additionally, the needs of a child will change over time, meaning that at one point in a child's academic career, the best environment might be home school. Yet at another point, private school may be the best option. Conversely, perhaps public school might be the best fit based upon what the local school offers. One size does not fit all.

Home education offers a tremendous amount of flexibility, especially for a child who struggles being in social situations. Yet, if you are a parent who finds yourself in constant conflict with your child or you find yourself dysregulated and unglued with your child's behavior most of the time, home schooling may not be the best option for your family until you have reached a better place in your own healing process.

There are many public schools that have tremendous resources available for children with special needs. However, most of the training public educators receive is based on behavioral modification. Finding a school in your community may take research and perseverance on your part. Do not be afraid to go up the food chain of administrators to advocate for your child's needs. I worked with one parent that went all the way to the governor's office!

Private schools can offer smaller classrooms with more one-on-one help. Many private schools specialize in helping children with difficult behaviors. Yet, some private schools can be more rigid in their structure and may not be a good fit for your child.

If you decide to put your child in school, use your intuition when you visit the school. How do you feel being there? Schools and teachers vary greatly. Just because a school is rated highly does not mean that it will be the best fit for your child.

Whichever avenue you choose for your child, remember that it is not permanent. If you decide to home school, you always have the option of going back into a different school environment if it does not work out well. My daughter was home schooled, then attended public school, and she is now in a private school. Each year her developmental stages vary, as do the schools and teachers available for her grade in a particular year.

Options are always available. The tragedy happens when parents lock themselves into a decision and feel as if they have to make it work or they have failed. Fear keeps us in the problem; love keeps us seeking solutions.

Q: *My daughter continues to struggle at school, yet we are relatively peaceful at home. It has gotten so bad that now my daughter is making herself vomit at school! The school staff has in the past reported that the violence, profanities, and threats are being done purposefully and their solution is to put her in a room by herself when she misbehaves. Now with the vomiting, they are talking about hospitalizing her. Yet, when I ask my daughter about all of this, she will say that she says things and vomits because it makes people angry and gets a reaction. The psychiatrist, who has diagnosed my daughter with RAD and PTSD (and possibly bipolar), feels that if she truly is saying things knowing what she's doing then we're dealing with something else. My question to you is, "Don't RAD kids do these things knowingly?"*

A: The basic understanding I want to encourage you to see is that the behaviors are flaring up because your daughter is getting stressed out. Whether it is bipolar, PTSD, RAD, etc, is not where we need to focus our attention. The violence, profanity, threats, and vomiting tells us that she is feeling threatened and feeling completely overwhelmed. She is fighting back in the only way she knows how. Your daughter is probably right on when she says that these behaviors get people angry and reactive. If she is feeling threatened, then she will want to be in control in order to provide safety for herself and fighting back is what we do as humans to gain some sense of control (think about the last time you yelled at her – you were most likely in a fear state trying to make things different at that very moment). Fighting back is a stress response rooted in fear so we need to work to understand what is causing her to shift into this emotional state of fear.

Your daughter will be able to tell you more about what is going on if she is given safe emotional space to do so. When she says she does this to make people angry, validate her in the sense that she must be very angry herself. Then continue to press through this behavior, "Something must be going on at school that makes you feel so threatened/so angry, sweetheart." Use your words with the goal of simply understanding what is driving her reactive and aggressive behaviors. Shift to the understanding that this behavior is only a communication of what is underneath it all.

As for the school, recognize that the school staff are feeling out of control themselves, thus putting the focus and blame back onto your daughter. This is so clear in their stating that if she does not straighten up then she will be placed in isolation, or hospitalized. Can you hear the fear in those options? The option of locking your daughter in a room by herself when she misbehaves is beyond conception and would certainly never address the core issues deep within your daughter's heart. It would only feed more fear and more stress into a body that is already at its maximum capacity.

Changing a behaviorally based paradigm within a school can be hard work, but it is not impossible. Continue to advocate, educate, and work with the school from a place of love, implementing the exact love-based paradigm you are proposing for your daughter. Remember that one person can make a difference.

Q: *Our children are only four and five. The older one does not do well every time we try to start preschool. She seems fine while at school and then we have a whole new set of challenges at home afterwards. She should be going to kindergarten next year, as she was five in January. I feel that she will not be able to handle it, as it is obviously a huge stressor for her and the rest of us after she goes to school. We have tried three different schools just one time each and haven't gone back. The latest school we tried three different times and always decided she wasn't ready. Help! The preschool teachers think I am nuts.*

A: Every child is uniquely designed and has different imprints from his or her past. Comparing a child to the "normal" child of the same age is dangerous because then you miss the individual needs and uniqueness of that child.

You stated that she "should be going to kindergarten." Let's look at this statement and ask ourselves, **who** determined that she should be going to kindergarten? Society? Standards? Baselines? None of these take into consideration the individual needs of your child.

I encourage you to "listen" to your child's behaviors. She is clearly telling you that she is not ready to handle the stress of the school environment. Allowing her the extra year to be with you will give her time to develop her regulatory system which will set her up for success in years ahead.

I also encourage you to trust your motherly instincts. You say she is not ready and you are right. Give yourself permission to meet your child at her emotional age, not her chronological age. You know your child best, so trust yourself. If the preschool teachers think you are nuts, then that is more about their lack of understanding as to the impact of trauma on the formative years of a child's life.

We often become more concerned about what others think than what is best for our child. Stop and take a few deep breaths and consider that statement. **Who is really the most important in this situation? Your child's emotional well-being or your reputation?**

You have already got what it takes to make this decision. Stay true to yourself and to the needs of your child.

Q: *My son, Daniel, now age four, has started tantruming since his sister started back to school in September. When I've questioned him about this, he says that he doesn't want his sister to go to school. I ask him if he is afraid when she goes to school, he says, "Yes" and he doesn't like it when she is gone. He did not have this trouble last year. We have tried a number of things to help him through this morning transition, including reviewing the morning schedule in the evening before he goes to bed so that the morning has no surprises. He is comfortable with the routine until it is time to get dressed and leave. This whole thing is very stressful for everyone and I don't know how to help him feel more comfortable and safe.*

A: Your mornings sound intense and extremely difficult. I would suspect that when you wake up in the morning, your first thoughts are on the lines of, "Oh, another morning to try to make things work." You would probably give anything to simply roll over and go back to sleep and take the morning off.

While your mornings have been difficult in the past and such thoughts are certainly understandable, the first step to breaking this negative loop comes at tomorrow's waking hour. Instead of dreading the requirements of the day, I want you shine more truth on the situation. "Daniel is terrified of his sister leaving for school this morning. Every morning previous to this morning, he has had to face this fear. What a challenge for him! He really does not know that his sister is going to come home and, at this point in his life, he feels incredibly insecure without her. I am 100% committed to helping him express his feelings around her leaving this morning."

Remind yourself that this is not about him rejecting you. Check in with yourself and see if there is not some negative self-talk like, "Am I not good enough for him?" and "Why can't he just be okay with the two of us together when his sister is not here?" or "I'm his mom. Why can't he feel as safe with me as he does with his sister?" Many times our internal dialogue, functioning from negative experiences and programs from the past, keeps us in a self-preservation mode, which constricts us from being able to give our children sympathy and understanding.

For Daniel, remember that healing happens in layers. What works one year may not work the next. Some interpret this change as regression; I see it as movement forward. While it was okay for his sister to be gone last year, it is not okay this year. Accepting that this is his natural, organic process is important in order to give him the flexibility to react one way at one time, then react another way at a different time.

It sounds like you are implementing all the right structure and that you are creating predictability for him. These, however, are all cognitive approaches to working out a deeply emotional issue. They work for awhile, then BOOM!, emotions go into overdrive and all the rational thought put into place is virtually useless at the moment of stress.

Fear has taken over. At this moment, he will need you to go deeper with him. He needs you to connect with the fear that is engulfing him at the moment. Here is what such an interaction might look like:

Mom: "Daniel, it is time to get dressed. I know that
          every morning when it is time to get dressed, it
          really scares you because that means that Sissy is

leaving for school. Today I want to help you with all that fear."

- *Validation*
- *Offer to stay in relationship*

Daniel: "I don't want her to go to school."

- *Following Daniel's lead.*
- *Helping Daniel identify the feeling behind the thought.*

Mom: "It is really hard when she goes to school, isn't it?"
Daniel: "I don't like it when she is gone."
Mom: "What does it feel like when she is gone?"

Daniel: "I don't know."

- *He probably doesn't know how to articulate this.*
- *Connecting with his fear of abandonment, rejection, etc.*
- *The real issue is starting to surface.*
- *Again, following Daniel's lead and working hard to connect with the core issue for Daniel.*
- *The invitation to express his emotions has just been sent.*

Mom: "Maybe when she's gone, it feels like she's never coming back."

Daniel: "Why does she get to go to school and I don't?"

Mom: "Is this what you're mad about?"

Daniel: "It's not fair."

Mom: "You're right. It isn't fair that you can't go to school. You have to watch while Sissy goes off to school and then you have come back home with me alone. This must make you really angry. Tell me you're mad. I need to know how hard this is for you!"
Daniel: "You're a stinky head and I'm mad you won't let me go to school."

- *You go, Daniel!*

Mom: "Give me more of your anger. Tell me at the top of your lungs how mad you are!"
Daniel: "I hate you."

- *Ignoring the behavior, but embracing the child.*
- *Reflection of how Daniel himself feels unlovable and hated.*
- *Affirming that he is being heard, giving permission to have his feelings.*

Mom: "I hear you, son. You have every right to be upset."

And the conversation keeps going until ultimately Daniel is given enough emotional space and reassurance to shift from anger to sadness. That is when Mom can move in to comfort him physically and softly tend to his pain.

Notice that the dialogue created by Mom in this example kept shifting Daniel back to the emotional issues. Rational thought and reasons why Daniel was not old enough to go to school were put on the back burner for later. **When talking with your children in the moment of their dysregulation, work to help them express their pain through feeling words (mad, sad, bad, etc.), not the details of the event.** Invite their emotional expression.

> ■
> *Validate. Affirm. Invite. Maximize instead of minimize. Keep the relationship intact, knowing that his feelings are not about you.*
> ■

Whether this is the underlying issue with Daniel, we do not know. Yet, the example gives a strategic process to follow with any issue. Dance with your child's conversation; let him take the lead. Know that you can go back after the storm has settled to talk about not using words such as "stinky head" and that you will have the opportunity to teach appropriate conversational skills when your child can actually listen to you. Validate. Affirm. Invite. Maximize instead of minimize. Keep the relationship intact, knowing that his feelings are not about you. Stay committed to the process and you will see that love never fails.

Classroom Methods for Teachers

Q: *(From a teacher). At the drop of a hat, one of my seven-year-old students will start yelling and crying. When I ask him what he is afraid of, he says me. I don't think I am really what he is afraid of because it can be that he has been given a piece of paper and he goes off. He made a snowman out of clay and when we were putting everyone's snowmen away, he just started yelling and crying. You can tell him that it is recess and he will yell that he doesn't want to go, but then he gets upset when everyone else leaves and he is still in the classroom. I know transitions are hard on him, but it seems he just doesn't know what he wants.*

A: I believe you have just answered your question by saying, "He just doesn't know what he wants." This child appears to be quite disorganized and disoriented. Are there not some days where you just feel like nothing is right and nothing is working? This child is living his entire existence in this state of dysregulation.

I would suspect that his history was chaotic and quite unpredictable. He has not been able to develop a sense of stability – yet. His internal self is still swirling around in a chaotic vortex.

As a teacher, recognize that it is not about the piece of paper or the snowman, or whatever happens to be the apparent trigger at the moment. He needs your help in modulating and handling the turmoil within himself.

When he starts yelling or crying, avoid any logical explanations as to why he will have to stop playing or why he will need to put his toys away. Simply acknowledge his emotions. "You're really upset, Billy. You have every right to be upset right now because that is exactly how you're feeling. Can you share those big feelings with me, sweetheart? They're too big to have all by yourself." Open your arms and see if he will be open to a hug or any type of appropriate physical touch. Physical touch can have a dramatic effect on helping to soothe a child in a dysregulated stated. Sometimes, however, touch can be overwhelming, so you will have to stay attuned to his cues.

He also might actually be afraid of you in the sense that he is afraid of adults in general. It is likely that his experiences of the past have put him in a place to fear you. When he says he is afraid of you, agree with him. "I see that you're afraid of me. I'm going to work really hard to make sure I'm a safe place for you." Put yourself in a place of physical safety, such as down on the floor or move back from him to give him some space. Do not leave him as this might ignite any abandonment issues, but ask him how you can be a safer place for him. He might even be able to give you some insight.

Remember that he wants your help, but his past experiences, based on the description of his behaviors, are giving him the feeling that if he accepts your help, you are going to hurt him. Stay focused on connecting with his emotional state and making yourself a safe place.

Q: *I am a teacher and after being introduced to your book this summer,* Beyond Consequences, Logic, and Control, *am wanting to incorporate these principles into my classroom. The book gives examples for parents, so I was hoping you could give some techniques for teachers in the classroom, as well.*

A: There are several ways to create a "Beyond Consequences Classroom." While I could give a list of techniques, there is only one place to start because a list of 100 techniques would be ineffective to creating a Beyond Consequences Classroom until one task is accomplished. And that begins with you. It begins in learning to see yourself in the moment. It is important to grasp the concept that the only thing that exists is now, at this moment. The next second does not exist and then, when the next second does arrive, it is not the next second anymore, it is now.

The reason this is so significant relates to stress. Stress causes us to either live out of the past or obsess about the future. Stress takes us out of the now. It is so easy for a teacher to miss making the connection with her student because the teacher is not present with the child. Here are a few stressors that can take the teacher out of the present: 1) the stress of past experiences with a difficult child, 2) the stress of feeling like a failure with a difficult child that triggers feelings of being a failure, 3) the fear of knowing that this child has the potential to feed his negativity into the entire class and create chaos amongst 25 other students, 4) the stress of "no child left behind" and the pressure of making certain that standardized state test scores are brought up from last year, 5) the triggering of past and uncon- scious memories of not being listened to in your childhood and feeling insignificant – feeling unworthy (all of which a seven-year-old child can do to you).

When you are out of the "here and now" because of any one of the above listed stressors, you will be reactive to the child and will not be able to respond in a way that helps the child calm his stress state. If you are becom- ing reactive to the child, then you are bringing something from your past or a fear of the future into the present. The child at that moment is behaving out of fear. Presenting yourself to that child in a fear state, as well, will only feed into the negative neurological feedback loop being created.

Conversely, coming into relationship with that child, knowing he is dysregulated rather than willfully being disobedient, and keeping yourself regulated and in the "now," will completely change the outcome. Engag- ing with that child with the goal of providing regulation for the child rather than disciplining the child will be more effective than any behavioral chart, token system, or removal of privileges. Such interactions will create a regu- lated and safe classroom, ideal for academic growth.

Stay present with each difficult child at that moment, connect with his fear state, create safety, and you will be helping the child learn how to regulate within the classroom setting.

Parent's Regulation

Q: *I listened to the Beyond Consequences Toddler audio CD and the topic of "how parents can learn to self-regulate" came up. I became VERY emotional. I was sobbing uncontrollably. My reactions to my child's negative behaviors are so immediate and ingrained. How do I get past this? I can't seem to find a good therapist in my area that under- stands the depth of my fear.*

A: A child living at a high level of stress and fear has the ability to open up a parent's own unresolved traumatic memories. While we resist this child's ability to open up our own dormant trauma, the truth is that this dynamic our child brings to us is an incredible gift in our midst.

A child living at a high level of stress and fear has the ability to open up a parent's own unresolved traumatic memories.

Working through these memories and experiences takes first courage, then the right resources, and lastly, commitment. Finding the courage within you is the key. It is scary to allow these past fears to come up to the surface after working so hard for so many years to keep them buried and "under control."

While individual therapy can help to work you through your pain from the past, sometimes it takes more intensive work. Much of my own healing came through participating in weekend intensive events and retreats. For a schedule of my events especially designed for mothers' healing and recovery, login to: www.EveryDayIsMothersDay.com.

Other ways to help you stay regulated include the following:

1. **Create a support system around you.** You need someone to turn to when you get dysregulated. Having someone simply listen to you, without trying to solve it all for you, can be golden.

2. **Devote time every day to contemplative prayer or meditation.** Creating a time to calm your nervous system everyday is critical to your well-being.

3. **Take care of yourself by working to find balance in your life.** Objectively look at pieces in your life that are creating more stress. You have permission to make the changes you need in your life, even if others do not agree with you. Be sure to make good nutrition and exercise a requirement of your lifestyle.

4. **Recognize that it is not your child's responsibility to love you.** This is your responsibility. Love and forgiveness are the most powerful regulatory "tools" we have as human beings. The BCI "Affirmations for Regulations" and Dare to Love Yourself audio CD's are a way to shift your own self love to a place of renewal and peace (www.beyondconsequences. com/shop.html). There is more information on this in *Beyond Consequences, Logic, and Control, Volume 2).*

5. **Address any marital issues that have not been resolved.** If your spouse is not loving you and relating to you in the way you need him/her, than you may subconsciously be looking for this through your children.

Find a marriage support group or seek marital therapy if needed.

6. **Develop a list of resources that help you find peace.** This may include such things as a bubble bath, listening to classical music, journaling, sketching, knitting, etc.

7. **Take responsibility for past relationships that are in tension, such as with a parent or a sibling.** Rise above the fray and apologize, ask for forgiveness, and let the past be the past. Remember that they may not be in a place to reciprocate a similar response, but you have done what you need to in order to move forward in your own life. You deserve to be able to move out of the past and it is your responsibility to move into a place of love within your life in the present and in the future.

8. **Breathe.** The quickest way to calm yourself in the moment is through **breathing.** It may seem like such a simple tool, but in times of stress, we typically stop breathing. Holding our breath only serves to exasperate and increase our stress level. Breathe in for a count of four, hold your breath for a count of seven, and breathe out for a count of eight. This is known as 4-7-8 breathing. Oxygen is always available to you and it is the most effective way to settle a nervous system.

9. **Take a time out.** If you get to a point of complete overwhelm and know that you are about to say something negative or act threatening to your child, **give yourself permission to take a time out.** Let your child know you are not leaving for good and that you are just going to your room for five minutes to calm down in order to be a better mommy or daddy.

10. **Forgive yourself**. Most importantly, **it takes forgiving yourself** for the way you have acted in relationship with your children in the past. For my own healing process, it took digging deep within me to forgive myself for being the most dysregulated mother on the planet. We come into our parenting roles with programs from our past. These programs put us in a place to act in a way that is based on our past experiences. So healing happens in this very moment by forgiving yourself and making a commitment to act differently next time. The only moment you have with your children is now, so letting the past be the past is the best place to find the regulation you are seeking.

You have it in you to make your world work for you and your family. It takes courage, tenacity, and 100% commitment. Anything is possible and I encourage you to keep pressing on with the vision of hope, healing, and peace.

Q: *I've read your books and everything you say makes so much sense to me. The problem that I have is being able to apply it. I get so caught up in my own stresses and fears that I seem to lose control more often than not. The result, of course, is that I am screaming and yelling at the children much too much. I know that I must help myself before I can help my precious children. I was wondering if you could address helping parents learn how to apply your methods.*

A: Applying the principles of the *Beyond Consequences* model is the most difficult task of all. I believe it takes reading and re-reading and re-reading my books and our other educational materials on the website (www.beyondconsequences.com). Yet, most importantly, it requires a deep understanding of ourselves and what we bring into the relationships with our children.

When you begin to feel your stress and fear rise to the surface, step back or sit down and start breathing and really connecting with what is going on inside of you. Feel it at a body level (Are my shoulders tight?, Is my stomach in a knot?, Is my jaw locked?). Trauma is stored at the body level, so when you begin to get stressed, these areas in the body will be activated.

Allow your feelings to surface (and know that this can be very painful). We frequently bypass our true feelings and emotional level of fear to instead, go straight to anger. It is much easier and less painful to be angry than it is to feel sadness or hopelessness. We have to remember that it is our own "bottom file drawer" that is being opened up (see *Beyond Consequences, Logic, and Control, Volume 1,* Chapter 5). This level of traumatic memory is more powerful than anything else within us.

The "state" level of memory overrides and supercedes our cognitive thinking. This is why we can have the best plans to do A-B-C the next time our children demonstrate negative behaviors, yet during that moment, we as parents do everything but our A-B-C plan. As you learn to connect with yourself at a body level, you are connecting with this state level of memory, which will increase your ability to remain attentive, attuned, and aware of the moment's dynamics.

Here is an example for you. One summer morning, my daughter was getting ready to go to camp. Historically, getting ready to leave the house had been a laborious and daunting task. Yet this morning, things were different. She was almost ready and we still had 30 minutes to spare. All she had to do was brush her teeth. Surely she could do this in 30 minutes while I focus on myself and get myself ready. Twenty-five minutes later though, I suddenly realize she is "floating" around the house and she still hasn't brushed her teeth.

In my mind, I immediately go into my reactionary and blaming state of, *"Can't I just get ready without having to stay on top of you every second?"* and *"I'm paying big bucks for this camp that YOU chose and*

YOU can't even get ready on time" and *"I've done everything for YOU this morning to make certain YOU get to camp on time and the only thing you have to do is simply brush your teeth!"* So, I yell. I get angry (not what my A-B-C plan had listed).

Then I stop and focus on my own piece of this. My stomach is in a knot. My arms **are** weak. I breathe and begin to find my own state of regulation. I calmly say to my daughter, as I start the car, "I want to get you there on time. My mother was always late. We were never able to make it to where I needed to be on time. We were constantly five or ten minutes late – always. When I was your age, I would try everything to help make it different so I could be on time. But no matter how hard I tried, it never worked." That was it! That was my feeling of being helpless in a situation that was identical to what was going on every morning during our getting ready routine. I was feeling helpless like when I was a little girl. Every morning my bottom file drawer was being opened up, which only went back to me feeling like I was not special enough for someone to finally take note of what I needed. This ultimately leads back to the fear of not feeling good enough for a parent and thus, fearful of not being secure in the parent-child relationship – the ultimate state of safety!

As I was able to understand myself, I was then emotionally open enough to see her fear. A light bulb went on in my head as I looked at her and felt her fear. I then said, "You're scared of leaving the house, aren't you honey?" Her history was that of leaving her birth home one morning and never returning. I could finally see her unconscious fear that was literally freezing her up so that she couldn't (not wouldn't, but couldn't) get ready to leave. She looked at me and said, "I'm scared that something is going to happen." So I sat there with her, validating her fear, soaking it all in so I would really know her story, and feeling the depth of pain within her. We eventually made it out the driveway and to camp. And it does not even matter if we were there on time or not!

Q: *I'm having a difficult time keeping myself focused on parenting in the Beyond Consequences way. I read your first two books and agree with them, but there are days that I feel like it is all for nothing. We have one good day where I think, "Great, this is it." Then the next three days we all are dysregulated and I feel discouraged. I keep telling my husband that I would rather go back to my full-time job, working 60 hours a week with deadlines due yesterday! Do you have any words of wisdom?*

A: A couple of days ago, I was attending a small group meeting and in order to introduce a few new members at this group, an ice breaker was given. We were asked to go around the room and in the spirit of Labor Day, tell not what we did for a living but what our parents did for a living when we were growing up. Several of the participants, after describing credentialed careers of high cultural status of their fathers, remarked, "But my mom was just a housewife."

Just a housewife! How sad I was to hear this coming from grown men and women who had their mothers home with them to support them, guide them, and teach them around the clock. Parenting is the most important job on this planet. You know this, I know this, but there has not been enough recognition in our society. Perhaps this is due to the intangible nature of this job. This job does not have a paycheck, there are no holiday bonuses, and there is no big desk to sit behind with plaques and certificates to recognize our accomplishments or to present our worth to others.

There is good news – this has changed. We are now living in a time where we can show real, tangible evidence of how important this job of parenting is for children. We now have solid, objective evidence that shows the need and importance of safe, attuned, and supportive parenting.

To give you an example, the image below shows the brain scans of two different three-year-olds. On the left side is a healthy three-year-old who has been in a nurturing and loving home his entire life. This child is showing an average size head (50th percentile). On the right side is a three-year-old who suffered severe sensory-deprivation neglect. This child's head is significantly smaller than average (3rd percentile). These images are taken from Dr. Bruce Perry's research ("Childhood Experience and the Expression of Genetic Potential: What Childhood Neglect Tells Us About Nature and Nurture." Brain and Mind 3: 79-100, 2002).

3-Year-Old Children

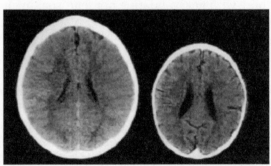

Normal   **Extreme Neglect**

While this example is extreme in nature, other examples of research are also showing the significance of nurturing care. Research is showing that simple changes in a child's environment can literally change a child's physiology. In a recent conversation with Dr. Karyn Purvis, I learned how their research at the TCU Institute of Child Development is demonstrating that by placing children with trauma histories in calmer environments with more love-based parenting techniques that are designed to create safety, stress hormones within these children's body systems are decreasing. This means that parents have the ability to literally change the chemical make-up of their children.

Certainly this is a job more powerful than the attorney next door or the mayor of your city. From the research today, our "job description" as parents is to help our children heal. While not an easy task, it is possible. It takes us changing our perspective not only to understand our children and ourselves, but a change in our understanding the significance of parenting. No more "just a housewife."

■

Our "job description" as parents is to help our children heal.

■

So, instead of waking up in the morning thinking, "I've got to get up, fix my children breakfast, pack their lunches, somehow get them off to school on time through the tantrums and meltdowns, and then prepare myself for the dreaded homework after school!" I encourage you to say to yourself, "Today is the day that I will press on to help change my child's brain. Today is the day that I have the ability to create life changing interactions with my child with understanding and loving support in order to help my child heal at a physiological and emotional level." Wow! Now that is something worth jumping out of bed for. Stay focused on the power you have through your relationship with your child.

Q: *I can "move in" to my daughter's vulnerability when she is hurting emotionally, but when she is disobedient and mean I do not want to "move in." Why? What holds me back?*

A: I want to first acknowledge you for your ability to distinguish at what points in your relationship with your daughter you feel safe and those that you do not. You are mindful enough to understand when you are able to "move in" and when you do not feel safe, but rather threatened. When feeling this threat, you are actually finding yourself against a wall – a barrier – that is preventing you from being able to "move in." Just the fact that you can make that significant distinction between the two is tremendous. You are a parent who is truly able to look at yourself in order to move forward in your ability to be the best parent you can be.

We need to look at the programs you have. Your program for emotional pain and upset defines this interaction as safe. When someone is upset, showing her emotions, crying, or showing her pain, you feel safe and you can stay in relationship. You can support that person. You can be there with her and know you are okay. This tells me that from your experiences in the past, which have created your present programs, you had someone supporting you. You were able to emote and they did not get angry back. The connection between emotional pain and relationship was very positive.

Now look at the flip side that says disobedience, meanness, cruelness, and anger are not safe, but instead are threatening. Being in relationship with those kinds of dynamics is an unsafe place for you to be. The program for disobedience in your family history and your earlier experiences appears to have resulted in pain, fear, discomfort, and/or disconnect.

If you do not feel safe being in the presence of someone who is mean, then you are not going to want to be connected with them. It is just like the little child who does not want to go into the haunted house because it is too scary. He is not going to want to go in, no matter how much his mother tries to convince him he will be okay. He is going to pull back. He is going to hide and do everything to fight against going into that place because it is a threat.

The same is true about relationships. To even think about moving into your daughter's disobedience or her place of dysregulation when she is mean is an unsafe place for you to go. I challenge you to reflect on your own previous experiences, whether they are childhood or early adult experiences where someone was disobedient or mean in your presence. Maybe it was a boss, an ex-boyfriend, your father, your mother, or an uncle who was mean and you did not feel safe. What happens now in the present is that at a body level you are programmed to experience fear when someone is mean. Your system does not know safety in these stressful times. Of course you do not want to "move in." That makes perfect sense.

However, as a parent it is our responsibility to "move in." The fear that you are experiencing is yours to overcome in order to connect with your daughter so that she does not develop similar programs. What an important understanding that as you overcome your barriers and are able to connect with her, you will not be transferring that type of generational fear-based programming.

The next time your daughter is mean or disobedient, I want you to take three deep breaths. I want you to reflect on where the pain is coming from in your body because that type of threat is going to show up at the body level. You may notice your chest tighten or your shoulders constricting. You may even notice your physical body actually backing up. Become mindful of what these bodily signals are because what we are working to do is to connect your mind with your body in order to bring them into unison.

As you are able to take three deep breaths, recognize and be aware of what your bodily reactions are. You can then unify your body/mind, through the power of the mind, and talk yourself into understanding that this is your daughter. This is not your uncle that used to yell at you or your ex-boyfriend who used to go into a tyrant. This is your daughter and she is hurting. If you can connect her disobedience and meanness to the equivalent of emotional pain, which is what it is, then you will find the ability to "move in" to the space with her and stay in relationship with her. Literally say to yourself, "This is not my father; this is my daughter." Separate past experiences from present experiences.

Breathing keeps us in the present. Breathing gives us the ability to override those old programs and make a conscientious, love-based decision to "move in" to and stay in relationship. Refer to Chapter 4, *Beyond Consequences, Logic, and Control, Volume 2,* for a discussion and example of how affirmations can assist in keeping you in the present moment.

When the Child Becomes a Parent

Q: *Reading the comments in one of the online chat rooms brings back such horrific memories of when I was doing my best to use Love and Logic while filled with my own fear. My daughter is now 20 and moved home from college because she was pregnant and now has her baby boy of three weeks in our house as well. About six months ago I found and read your book, "Beyond Consequences, Logic, and Control." It made such an unbelievable difference in our relationship, and I have done soul searching as well.*

My question is, to what extent am I the "calming" I'll-never-leave-you-mother while she sometimes acts like a 13-year-old and to what extent do I encourage her to differentiate from me and face "consequences" of huge responsibilities with finances, mothering her baby, school decisions, etc.?

A: It sounds like she is indeed about 13 years old, emotionally. I would suggest parenting her as if she is 13 years old because that is all she can be right now. The stress of being a mother at a young age with financial issues and other concerns is understandably overwhelming her. As you take responsibility for much of this, she will learn to eventually do it on her own. Yet, allowing your daughter to stay in a state of overwhelm will not give her the space to grow and improve.

If it takes being home for several years, that is just what it might take.

■ *Allowing your daughter to stay in a state of overwhelm will not give her the space to grow and improve.* ■

This will allow her the opportunity to grow so when she does eventually go back on her own, she will be able to make it successfully. Plus, this gives you a chance to create the relationship you two did not have in the past.

Additionally, by re-parenting your daughter, you are giving her the tools and the experiential knowledge of how to now parent her own child. You cannot give that which you have not received. Now that your daughter is able to receive your love, she will be more equipped to give back love unconditionally to her child. You have the power within you at this very moment to change the next generation within your home. What a gift!

Remember that nothing has the capacity to produce real change like real love.

Biblical Perspective

Q: *As a Christian, how do I "let go" or overlook some of the bad behaviors? Sometimes, it is very hard to overlook the behaviors that I know are true sins, such as being disrespectful and using foul language. It is clear in the Bible that these are sins. So, how do I get where I can go with the love based approach and be "okay" with overlooking these behaviors at times? I understand it and believe in it, but I still have a hard time dealing with some of this at times. Any suggestions?*

A: Sin is about being outside of God's love. If we're outside of God's love, we are in a state of fear. *"There is no fear in love. But perfect love drives out fear, because fear has to do with punishment. The one who fears is not made perfect in love." (1 John 4:18).* The question then becomes, how do you shift back into a state of love?

To "let go" of these behaviors means to understand these behaviors and to recognize your responsibility as a parent to teach your child how to shift back. Being a Beyond Consequences parent give you the permission to demonstrate unconditional love through patience, acceptance, tolerance, and understanding. Correlating this to Biblical examples, the Gospel is overflowing with examples of how Christ helped to shift the "sinful" back into communion with God through love, not fear.

Scripture also demonstrates the principle of discipling, showing us that the purpose of discipline is to teach. The word discipline comes from the Latin word "disciplina" from "discipulus" or simply, "pupil". Unfortunately, our cultural and worldly understanding of this definition has become distorted to mean to "punish." If we look at Scriptural examples of discipline or disciple, it is clearly shown that this process of learning is with gentleness, safety, and peacefulness. *"Come to me, all you who labor and* *are heavily burdened, and I will give you rest. Take my yoke upon you, and **learn from me, for I am gentle and lowly in heart;** and you will find rest for your souls. For my yoke is easy, and my burden is light."* (Matthew 11:28-30).

With this understanding of discipline, children learn to regulate through a safe, loving, and meaningful relationship. They learn to respect others, not from a place of fear, but from a place of love. As they are fully and unconditionally accepted through mistakes or poor decisions, they can change and modify their behaviors without shame, blame, or fear of punishment. This type of loving environment opens the doors for exponential growth in children. Unconditional love provides a foundation for a life free of limitation, lack, and scarcity. Abundance of love and forgiveness is far more powerful than consequences and control.

One specific lesson that discipline teaches is responsibility. Again, the world has distorted this understanding of responsibility and has shifted the responsibility onto even our youngest of children. The philosophy of, "If they don't learn to be responsible now, even in kindergarten, then they'll never learn to take responsibility." Do you hear the fear in that statement? The truth is that children learn through modeling. As parents take responsibility for themselves and then for their children, this pattern becomes instilled in the children. Seeing adults take responsibility teaches children to take responsibility.

Discipline is also an opportunity to develop strong relationships between parents and children. We see a great example of this in Scripture: *"But he said to me, 'My grace is sufficient for you, for my power is made perfect in weakness.'"* (2 Corinthians 12:9). It is in our children's weakness, that we have the opportunity to support them, love them, and provide our influence (not power) as parents to build them back up again. As they learn to regulate through the parent/child relationship, they learn to connect with others outside their family. They develop the ability as young adults to develop healthy relationships that are void of manipulation, control, and conditions.

> ∎
> *Abundance of love and forgiveness is far more powerful than consequences and control.*
> ∎

The book of Romans provides numerous examples of a love-based parenting paradigm. *"If your enemy is hungry, feed him; if he is thirsty, give him something to drink."* (Romans 12:20). And thus, if your child is acting out, give him attention. If he is talking back and rejecting your directives, connect with him instead of rejecting him in return with consequences. If he is picking on his sibling, provide your reassurance in his place in the family instead of ostracizing him in time-out.

The most concise example is when Paul writes, *"Do not be overcome by evil, but overcome evil with good." (Romans 12:21)*. Taking the liberty to put this in the context of parenting, we can say that, "Do not be overwhelmed by negative behavior, but overcome negative behavior with love."

It first takes loving, forgiving, and accepting yourself in order to be empowered to do the same for your children.

Foster Children

Q: *In your books, you mention that the parent should calm a child down by creating security for the child. My children are foster children so much of their stress and fear comes from the threat of being moved to another home. Yet as a foster mom, I can never honestly say, "You are safe. You aren't going anywhere."*

A: You are absolutely right. You would never want to say this to a foster child because the reality is that they probably will be moving on to another home in the future.

What you have working for you is the present moment. The only moment we have guaranteed to us is the moment we are in. Capture this moment with your child. Say to her, "You are safe, honey. You are right here with me now." You can give security and nurturing at that moment. Help your child learn how to stay present with you in this precious space in time.

I recently had a foster mother relate a story to me that will help you understand the power of even short term loving relationships. This foster mother had a teenage foster child in her home for a period of only one month. Eight years later, after the child had aged out of the system and was on her own as an adult, she and the foster mother reconnected. The former foster child told this foster mother that the turning point in her life was when she was at her home. The love, safety, security, and acceptance that she was given by this foster mother changed her life and gave this former foster child the ability to move forward. She relayed how this placement, only one month in length, was the best placement she had EVER had.

You are an important part of your foster child's journey. Never underestimate the importance of your time with her, whether it is short or long term, and your ability to create safety and security in each moment, despite an uncertain future.

Q: *How do you give a narrative to a child that suffered neglect as an infant during the first three months of his life, especially when I do not know the details?*

A: Children need to know their stories. This helps them understand themselves and gives them an understanding of who they are.

The actual details of the story are not important, and in fact, should not be the focus. This is especially true for trauma that happened preverbally (before the child was speaking). Infants and young children are 100% emotional beings, so the story needs to be told from this level to connect with the child's early experiences.

When giving your child his story, focus on how the child felt (helpless, scared, terrified, sad, hungry, etc.). A child who was neglected missed the warm and nurturing touch of a parent, so hold your child next to you or in your lap while giving him his story.

The important factors are your tone of voice, facial expressions, posture, and tempo of movement and speech. These are all right brain expressions that will speak to the subconscious experiences of your child.

Dr. Allan Shore, the "king" of affect regulation, explains that the right brain is the unconscious processor of the emotional self. The attachment bond is an emotional bond, so it takes expressing yourself and your child's story at the emotional level. What you say is not as important as how you say it.

A dialogue might sound something like this:

"When you were a little baby, sweetheart, you were really scared. Your mommy wasn't able to help you like you needed her to. There were many times that you were left in your crib alone. Babies get super scared when this happens because they are helpless. I'm certain this is how you were feeling. It probably felt like you weren't lovable, also. I do wish I could have been there. I'm so sorry this happened to you, honey."

■

The paradox is that in order to move forward, it takes going backwards, seeing the fullness of the fear and pain and experiencing it at all levels.

■

I was speaking to a mother just the other day about giving her daughter who was severely neglected for the first year of her life her story. The mother's fear prompted these questions, "Do you think that this will just make it worse for her? Won't this only bring up bad memories and get her upset?"

This is an understandable fear that parents have, You are simply trying to get better and move on in your healing process yet I am suggesting a trip back in time to expose the pain and overwhelm. The paradox is that in order to move forward, it takes going backwards, seeing the fullness of the fear and pain and experiencing it at all levels.

When your child's story goes unexpressed, he will be subconsciously living it out everyday. This pain and overwhelm will continue to influence him and drive him in his actions. You are not giving him anything new by giving him his story. You are simply bringing the subconscious to the conscious so it does not have the power to create dysregulation anymore. When these stories, connected to the feelings and emotions, can be expressed, healing happens.

Clean out the closet to make room for joy, happiness, peace, and love!

So the question then becomes, "Whose fear is this really about?" Resistance is about the parent's fear of going back to experience the depth of darkness that her child experienced. Just the thought of what some of our children went through is completely overwhelming to us.

I remember one day my daughter, who was also severely neglected, was beginning to open up to her early life experiences. I was getting so overwhelmed by her pain that I had to call a friend over to be with me so I could stay present with her. I needed support. Interesting that it was too much for me as an adult, so why is it that we expect our children to live alone in this kind of pain by themselves and be okay?

Find the courage to experience your child's early life with him, feel the impact of his feelings of being unworthy, and validate how bad it was for him. Then, you will have opened up the space for healing and a connected and happy future.

Remember that attachment is about decreasing negative emotions. But even more than that, attachment is about increasing positive emotions. Clean out the closet to make room for joy, happiness, peace, and love!

Q: *My foster son is 14 years old and has been in our home for two years. Since being with us, he has been sporadic in his sleep habits, but in the last year, it has gotten worse. His eating patterns are chaotic and he just seems completely out of balance. I'm trying to keep a regular and predictable schedule for him but this just isn't working.*

A: For any teenager, and especially for teenagers with traumatic histories, their circadian rhythms are disrupted. Circadian rhythms are the daily rhythms in the body that keep you balanced at a physiological level. They help you wake up and calm you down around sleep, they give you indicators as to when to eat, and they provide several other sensory experiences.

Circadian rhythms are naturally disrupted during the teenage years. For your foster son with a traumatic history, these rhythms were disrupted even before becoming a teenager due to environmental stressors, which means that now, during his teenage years, they are intensely disrupted.

The result is a son who needs to sleep at all hours of the day, eats in an unpredictable fashion, and simply operates in a disrupted physiological state. It is not a choice for him. **It is simply how his body is operating at this developmental stage in his life; it is his inherent biological rhythm.**

Parenting him will take understanding this biological principle. The next time your son has a hard time waking up at six o'clock in the morning, realize that his biological clock is telling him to sleep until noon. This is not resistance or defiance. It is simply how he is programmed at this stage in his life. Having this understanding will give you more patience and allow you to support him more as he struggles through life right now.

When trying to wake him up, tell him you understand how hard it must be for him. Many times we are so rushed in the morning that we focus solely on the logistics of getting ready, eating breakfast, and getting to the bus on time. **Take a few minutes to connect with him, offer understanding, and allow him emotional space to be grumpy and resistant.** As you focus on staying in relationship with him, he will have a greater ability to respond to you in a positive way when you ultimately have to say, "Okay, honey, we really have to get going now."

Do some research on circadian rhythms and share it with him. Perhaps he will even sit down with you at the computer when you google this information. When he sees you taking interest in understanding him, it will speak volumes to him. **As he begins to understand what is going on within his own body, he won't have to feel as if there is something wrong with him.**

Of course, as with most teenagers, he will be clever to use this in his favor. When you need him to get up and go to school, his response might be something like, "I can't get up. It's my circadian rhythms!" This is where you have a brilliant opportunity to teach him how to not fall into being a victim to his biology. **Through the power of his mind, he has the ability to overcome even the toughest of obstacles.** As a foster child, I am certain he has had numerous experiences of feeling powerless. Empower him to take back his personal power and make his life work for him.

You mentioned you have been setting a schedule, which can sometimes be helpful. A scheduled external world can influence a child's "internal world" to become more regular. There is however, a clarification I want to add to this. There is a huge difference between predictable schedule and rigid schedule. Too often, parents create a schedule for their family, yet set it into stone. This creates a rigid environment with little tolerance for the smallest variation. Rigidity is the first sign of death! So set a schedule, but in moderation allow for flexibility.

Yet, you mentioned that this has not helped. Your son may need to set his own schedule. Empower him to take charge of his body by having him set up a schedule for himself. If he feels as if he has some control over his daily life, he will be more motivated. **No one likes being told what to do and when to do it, especially teenagers.**

There are certain "must-do" events in everyday that he will not have control over (such as when to be at school, when to be at basketball practice, etc.). Yet, the other times of the day, help him learn how to plan out his daily life. Besides helping him to feel like he has some control over his life, you are teaching him a valuable tool that many adults have yet to master. Some teens may be too dysregulated to follow the actual plan, but you are at least helping them to begin the process and it is giving him time to process ahead of time his daily life.

Most importantly, **when you stay in a place of understanding, decreasing the level of frustration you bring into your interactions with him, you are providing a healthier and safer environment within the context of your relationship with him.** This is the most effective "tool" you have available. Your loving influence, wrapped with understanding, will help him establish more consistent rhythms within his body.

Q: *Your daily reflection stated, "In order for children to open up to their past trauma memories, the parent has to be willing to be a 'parental sponge' – acknowledging, absorbing, and experiencing every feeling, every tear, and every fear associated with the trauma. Now that is connection!" My concern is this: Experiencing your child's or client's trauma at such an intensity, couldn't that create trauma for the person being the 'sponge'? I feel I am very empathic but how can I do that without hurting myself?*

A: This is an insightful question. Traditionally, most of us are empathic and give compassion in a way that ultimately drains us. This is because of a core belief that tells us that by giving empathy, we will be able to make this person better or that we have the ability to "fix" the problem for this person.

We own that it is up to us to get this person to shift into a calm, peaceful, and regulated state. Their issue then becomes our issue and we stay focused on the outcome of them being better.

It becomes a simple mathematical equation. If I give empathy (E), if I listen (L), and if I spend my time with this person (T), he will be better (B). E + L + T = B

Yet, when we give these three and the result is not what we expected, we feel a sense of failure. We turn it back on ourselves and hear the old negative tapes playing in our head, "I didn't try hard enough." "I'm not good enough." "I should have done something differently." BAM! The negative feedback loop then feeds on itself right within our own mind. Fatigue, overwhelm, and even resentment begin to brew within our internal selves.

> ■
> *Conditional love is draining. Unconditional love is energizing and liberating.*
> ■

In order to be a sponge, the only action we need to take is to simply be present with our child *(or friend, spouse, coworker)*. It is not up to us to make this person better. The reality is that we cannot change or fix another person. We can surround them with support; we can love them unconditionally, free of judgment or control; we can set appropriate boundaries, and we can align with their pain. Yet in doing this, it is still ultimately up to them to make their life work.

Additionally, if we enter into an interaction with a child, expecting him to be better, we are actually adding more stress to the equation, which will create more fear and hinder the healing process. We must stay focused on giving our love without expecting anything in return. That is the essential definition of love.

Entering into an interaction with an expectation of an outcome is not true love. This is conditional love. Conditional love drains us. Unconditional love energizes and liberates us.

So that is the theory and I know you are reading this and wanting some meat to chew on – you want application to your 16-year-old teenager whose girlfriend just dumped him and he is feeling like the entire world is coming to an end. You see how his past abandonment issues are being triggered and how this situation is being magnified due to his early history.

Reprogram your thinking to see that what he needs is your support, your attention, and your unconditional acceptance. It is not up to you to make this okay for him. Trust that it is in the struggles of life that we learn and grow to our maximum potential.

By being empathetic, by listening, by spending time, and being present with him you are doing EVERYTHING for him. Stay focused on the outcome of you being the absolutely best parent you can be, no matter the outcome of his emotional state at the moment. Your "success" cannot be tied to his feeling better instantaneously.

Keep being the sponge for your child's pain. Become energized by the power of putting unconditional love into action. There is no greater state to be in on this planet!

Recommended Readings

■

Resources for Parents:

Brazelton, T.B. (1992). *Touchpoints: Your child's emotional and behavioral development*. Reading, MA: Addison-Wesley Publishing.

Brazelton, T.B. & Greenspan, S. (2000). *The irreducible needs of children: What every child must have to grow, learn, and flourish*. Cambridge, MA: Perseus Publishing.

Breggin, P. (2000). *Reclaiming our children: A healing solution for a nation in crisis*. Cambridge, MA: Perseus Books.

Chopra, D. (1994). *Journey into healing*. New York: Harmony Books.

Clark, N. & Post, B. (2005). *The forever child: A tale of loss and impossible dreams*. Mountain View, OK: M. Brynn Publishing.

Clark, N. & Post, B. (2003). *The forever child: A tale of fear and anger*. Mountain View, OK: M. Brynn Publishing.

Clark, N. & Post, B. (2002). *The forever child: A tale of lies and love*. Mountain View, OK: M. Brynn Publishing.

Covey, S.R. (2007). *The 8th habit: From effectiveness to greatness*. New York, NY: Free Press.

Davis, P. (1999). *The power of touch: The basis for survival, health, intimacy, and emotional well-being*. Carlsbad, CA: Hay House.

Eldridge, S. (1999). *Twenty things adopted kids wish their adoptive parents knew*. New York, NY: Dell Publishing.

Forbes, H.T. & Post, B.B. (2006). *Beyond consequences, logic, and control: A love-based approach to helping attachment-challenged children with severe behaviors,* Volume I. Boulder, CO: BCI.

Forbes, H.T. (2008). *Beyond consequences, logic, and control: A love-based approach to helping attachment-challenged children with severe behaviors,* Volume 2. Boulder, CO: BCI.

Forbes, H.T. & Dziegielewski, S. (2003). *Issues facing adoptive mothers of children with special needs*. Journal of Social Work 3 (3). (Available for download at: www.beyondconsequences.com)

Goldman. D. (2006). *Social Intelligence*. New York, NY: Bantam Books.

Goleman, D. (1994). *Emotional intelligence: Why it can matter more than IQ*. New York, NY: Bantam Books.

Granju, K. & Kennedy, B. (1999). *Attachment parenting: Instinctive care for your baby and young child*. New York, NY: Pocket Books.

Hanh, T. (1987). *Being peace*. Berkeley, CA: Parallax Press.

Harris, B. (2008). *Confident parents, remarkable kids: 8 principles for raising kids you'll love to live with*. Avon, MA: Adams Media.

Harris, B. (2003). *When your kids push your buttons and what you can do about it*. New York, NY: Warner Books.

Hanessian, L. (2004). *Let the baby drive: Navigating the road of new motherhood*. New York, NY: St. Martin's Press.

Hart, A. (1992). *Stress and your child*. Dallas, TX: Word Publishing.

Jamplosky, G. (1979). *Love is letting go of fear*. Berkley, CA: Celestial Arts.

Karen, R. (1994). *Becoming attached: Unfolding the mystery of the infant-mother bond and its impact on later life*. New York, NY: Warner Books, Inc.

Karr-Morse, R., & Wiley, M.S. (1997). *Ghosts from the nursery: Tracing the roots of violence*. New York: Atlantic Monthly Press.

Kohn, A. (2006). *The homework myth: Why our kids get too much of a bad thing*. Cambridge, MA: Da Capo Press.

Kohn, A. (2005). *Unconditional parenting: Moving from rewards and punishment to love and reason*. New York, NY: Atria Books.

Kranowitz, C.S. (2006). *The out-of-sync child: Recognizing and coping with sensory processing disorde*. New York, NY: Penguin Group.

Liedloff, J. (1986). *The continuum concept*. New York, NY: Penguin Books.

Perry, B. & Szalavitz M. (2007). *The boy who was raised as a dog: And other stories from a child psychiatrist's notebook – What traumatized children can teach us about loss, love, and healing*. New York, NY: Basic Books.

Rosenberg, M. (2003). *Nonviolent communication: A language of life*. Encinitas, CA: Puddle Dancer Press.

Sears, W. & Sears, M. (2001). *The attachment parenting book: A commonsense guide to understanding and nurturing your baby*. New York, NY: Little, Brown and Company.

Selye, H. (1974). *Stress without distress*. New York, NY: Signet.

Siegel, D. & Hartzell, M. (2003). *Parenting from the inside-out: How a deeper self-understanding can help you raise children who thrive.* New York, NY: Jeremy P. Tarcher/ Putnam.

Tolle, E. (1999). *The power of now.* Novato, CA: New World Library.

Verrier, N.N. (1993). *The primal wound: Understanding the adopted child.* Baltimore, MD: Gateway Press.

Additional Resources for Professionals:

Bowlby, J. (1988). *A secure base: Parent-child attachment and healthy human development.* New York, NY: Basic Books.

Bowlby, J. (1980). *Attachment and loss: Vol. 3 Loss: Sadness and depression.* New York: Basic Books.

Bowlby, J. (1973). *Attachment and loss: Vol. 2 Separation and anger.* New York, NY: Basic Books.

Bowlby, J. (1969). *Attachment and loss: Vol.1 Attachment.* New York, NY: Basic Books.

Bremner, J. (2002). *Does stress damage the brain?: Understanding trauma-related disorders from a mind-body perspective.* New York, NY: W.W. Norton and Company.

Carnegie Corporation (1994). *Starting point: Meeting the needs of our youngest children: The report of the Carnegie task force on meeting the needs of young children.* New York, NY: Carnegie Corporation of New York.

DeGangi, Georgia. (2000). *Pediatric disorders of regulation in affect and behavior.* New York, NY: Academic Press.

Frattaroli, E. (2001). *Healing the soul in the age of the brain.* New York, NY: Penguin Books.

Greenspan, S., and Cunningham, A. (1993, August 22). *Where do violent kids come from?* Charlotte Observer, reprinted in the Washington Post.

Janus, L. (1997). *Echoes from the womb.* Livingston, NY: Jason Aronson.

Justice, B., & Justice, R. (1990). *The abusing family.* New York, NY: Plenum Press.

Kandel, E.R. (1998). *A new intellectual framework for psychiatry.* American Journal of Psychiatry, 155, 457-469.

LeDoux, J. (1996). *The emotional brain: The mysterious underpinnings of emotional life.* New York, NY: Touchstone.

Levine, P.A. (1999). *Healing trauma: Restoring the wisdom of the body.* (Audio Cassette Recording). Louisville, CO: Sounds True, Inc.

Levine, P.A. (1997). *Waking the tiger, healing trauma.* Berkley, CA: North Atlantic Books.

Lipton, B. (2005). *The biology of belief: Unleashing the power of consciousness, matter, and miracles.* Santa Rosa, CA: Mountain of Love/Elite Books.

McEwen, B.S. (1992). Paradoxical effects of adrenal steroids on the brain: Protection vs. degeneration. *Biological Psychiatry 31,* 177-199.

McEwen, B. (1999). Development of the cerebral cortex XIII: Stress and brain development – II. *Journal of the American Academy of Child and Adolescent Psychiatry, 38,* 101-103.

Montagu, A. (1986). *Touching: The human significance of the skin.* New York, NY: Harper and Row.

National Center for Clinical Infant Programs (2005). *Diagnostic classification of mental health and developmental disorders of infancy and early childhood.* Arlington, VA: Zero to Three.

Perry, B.D. (2002). Childhood experience and the expression of genetic potential: What childhood neglect tells us about nature and nurture. *Brain and Mind, 3,* 79-100.

Perry, B.D. & Pollard, R. (1998). Homeostasis, stress, trauma and adaptation: A neurodevelopmental view of childhood trauma. *Child and Adolescent Psychiatric Clinics of North America, 7*(1) 33-51.

Perry, B.D. (1997). Incubated in terror: Neurodevelopmental factors in the "cycle of violence." In J. Osofsky (Ed.), *Children in a violent society* (pp. 124-149). New York, NY: Guilford Press.

Perry, B.D. (1996). *Maltreated children: Experience, brain development, and the next generation.* New York, NY: W. W. Norton.

Perry, B.D. (1996). *Neurodevelopmental adaptations to violence: How children survive the intergenerational vortex of violence, Violence and childhood trauma: Understanding and responding to the effects of violence on young children,* Gund Foundation, Cleveland.

Perry, B.D., Pollard, R.A., Blakely, T.L. Baker, W.L., & Vigilante, D. (1995). Childhood trauma, the neurobiology of adaptation, and "use-dependent" development of the brain: How states become traits. *Infant Mental Health Journal, 16,* 271-291.

Perry, B.D. (1993). Neurodevelopment and the neurophysiology of trauma: Conceptual considerations for clinical work with maltreated children. *The Advisor, American Professional Society on the Abuse of Children, 6:1.*

Pert, C.B. (2004). *Your body is your subconscious mind* (Audio CD Recording). Louisville, CO: Soundstrue, Inc.

Pert, C.B. (2004). *Psychosomatic wellness: Healing your bodymind* (Audio CD Recording). Magic Bullets, Inc.

Pert, C.B. (1997). *Molecules of emotion.* New York, NY: Touchstone.

Ross, C.A. (2000). *The trauma model.* Richardson, TX: Manitou Communications.

Sapolsky, R.M. (1990). Stress in the wild. *Scientific American 262,* 116-23.

Scaer, R.C. (2005). *The trauma spectrum: Hidden wounds and human resiliency.* New York, NY: W.W. Norton & Company, Inc.

Schore, A.N. (1994). *Affect regulation and the origin of the self.* Hillsdale, NJ: Lawrence Erlbaum Associates, Publishers.

Schore, A.N. (2003). *Affect regulation and the repair of the self.* New York, NY: W.W. Norton.

Shapiro, F. & Forrest, M. (1998). *EMDR: The breakthrough therapy for overcoming anxiety, stress, and trauma.* New York, NY: Basic Books.

Siegel, D.J. (1995a). Memory, trauma, and psychotherapy: A cognitive science view. *Journal of Psychotherapy Practice and Research, 4,* 93-122.

Solomon, M.F. & Siegel, D.J. (Eds.). (2003). *Healing trauma: Attachment, mind, body, and brain.* New York, NY: W.W. Norton & Company.

Index
∎

Order Form

■

Books	Quantity	Cost	Total
Beyond Consequences, Logic, and Control: *A Love-Based Approach to Helping Attachment-Challenged Children with Severe Behaviors*			

    1 to 4 copies: $19.95 each
    5 to 10 copies: $17.95 each
    11 to 25 copies: $15.95 each
    26 to 50 copies: $13.95 each
    (Prices good for both Volumes 1 and 2)

Dare to Love
    (Prices same as above)

100 Daily Parenting Reflections *A Love-Based Parenting Nuggets to Encourage You Daily*
    $9.95 each

DVD

Beyond Consequences Live!
4-set DVD
If you've been unable to attend a Beyond Consequences Live training event, here is your solution. Intensive role plays on this dynamic DVD will give you "real-life" examples to equip you as a parent with "real-life" solutions.
    $109.00 each

Audio CD's

Beyond Consequences for **Toddlers, 5 to 9's, Tweens, Teenagers**
9-disc Audio CD Set
This 9-part audio CD set will bring you solutions and to a deeper understanding of the books *Beyond Consequences, Logic, and Control.* These discussions hit the mark for children of all ages and put the concepts of this book into action.
    Price: $97.00

Shipping Costs _____

Total Cost _____

Payable to:

Beyond Consequences Institute
1630A 30th Street, #488
Boulder, CO 80301
www.beyondconsequences.com

Shipping and Handling Scale:
up to $25.00 .... $ 5.95.
$25.01 - $45.00 .... $ 7.95
$45.01 - $90.00 .... $ 9.95
$90.01 - 140.00 .... $ 12.95
$140.01 - 190.00 .... $ 14.95
$190.01 - 240.00 .... $ 16.95
$240.01 - 290.00 .... $ 18.95
over $290.01 .... please call

About the Author
■

Heather T. Forbes, LCSW

Heather T. Forbes, LCSW, is the owner of the Beyond Consequences Institute. She is an internationally published author on the topics of adoptive motherhood, raising children with difficult and severe behaviors, and self-development. Forbes lectures, consults, and coaches parents throughout the U.S., Canada, Europe, and Australia. She supports families in crisis working to create peaceful, loving families. Forbes is passionate about supporting families by bridging the gap between academic research and "when the rubber hits the road" parenting. Much of her experience and insight on understanding trauma, disruptive behaviors, developmental delays, and adoption-related issues comes from her direct mothering experience of her two internationally adopted children.